VIA DIPLOMATIC POUCH

BY DOUGLAS MILLER

You Can't Do Business With Hitler

Via Diplomatic Pouch

By

DOUGLAS MILLER

With a Foreword by William L. Shirer

DIDIER

New York

INTRODUCTION

IF ANY CITIZEN of this country has the right to stand up and say: "I told you so"—it is Douglas Miller.

He began warning his fellow-Americans about the threat of Nazism long before Hitler came to power. At that time it was like crying in the desert. Even as late as June, 1941, just six months before Hitler declared war on us, there were many who were skeptical of his book published that month, *You Can't Do Business with Hitler.* That excellent book was addressed primarily to American businessmen, whom Mr. Miller had served so well (though few of them realized it) during fifteen years in the United States Embassy in Berlin. In a preface to the book he wrote: "There is one group in America which has not been adequately brought face to face with the facts. I mean American businessmen."

Even at that time—six months before Pearl Harbor and the German declaration of war—it was not Mr. Miller's fault. As our commercial attaché in Berlin he had been trying to tell American businessmen the truth about Nazism from its very inception.

Each year he wrote a review of the economic situation in Nazi Germany. These annual reviews were little masterpieces. He sent them off to Washington where, I'm afraid, they were buried by the bureaucracy. This was an unfortunate and unpardonable mistake. I once urged Ambassador Dodd to pressure the State Department or the Commerce Department or President Roosevelt or God to get them published. I believe he did, but without success.

Fortunately—I think I can reveal this now—some of Mr. Miller's material did get into print over the dead body of sleepy Washington. I don't suppose it was according to the antiquated government rules, but Mr. Miller did entrust, in confidence, copies of his annual report on Germany to a handful of us correspondents in Berlin. We used his material time and again in our dispatches. I have before me three of these yearly reviews which I brought back from Germany. They are well thumbed and they will continue to be thumbed.

Now at long last—better late than never—some of these reports are made available in this book for the American people. Since the annual reviews of Germany were rather long and full of statistical material Mr. Miller has decided to publish only shorter confidential reports dealing with particular topics which would seem to be of most interest to the reading public. All of us, especially our businessmen, some of whom were done in so thoroughly by the Germans, will profit by reading them. Whether we like it or not we shall probably always have Germans on this earth to deal with. These fine reports of Mr. Miller's will help us all in this difficult task.

WILLIAM L. SHIRER

TABLE OF CONTENTS

	PAGE
Introduction by William L. Shirer	v
Preface	ix

CHAPTER

1. National Socialism *vs.* American Business — 13
2. Economic Program of the National Socialists — 20
3. Autarchy — 23
4. "Gleichschaltung" — 31
5. The "Organic Society" — 37
6. The "Estates" — 42
7. Growing Radicalism — 47
8. Changes and Decrees — 52
9. Consolidation of Nazi Positions — 59
10. Campaign Against Unemployment and Foreign Goods — 64
11. American Business Interests in Germany — 71
12. Hitler and the Stability of Eastern Europe — 79
13. Racial "Theories" and Legislation — 88
14. National Socialist Movement at the End of 1933 — 98
15. Economic Ideas — 106
16. New German Labor Code — 116

CONTENTS

CHAPTER   PAGE

17. Industry Under the Nazis   125

18. Business Relations with the United States   133

19. Sidelights on the Situation   165

20. Foreign-Exchange Blockade   171

21. New System of Import Control   189

22. Control Offices and Our Trade with Germany   198

23. Raw-Material Outlook   207

24. Facing the Facts   213

25. Regulations of July 29 and American Companies   222

26. Expropriation of Jewish Enterprises   227

27. Hitler's Dilemma   236

    Bibliography on "Racial Science"   247

PREFACE

At the suggestion of Mr. J. P. Didier I have collected for publication in a single volume a number of reports which I wrote in Berlin, Germany, beginning with the year 1931 when it became evident that Hitler was going to gain power. In every case the date has been given. Nothing new has been added and few changes have been made in the text, chiefly improvements in punctuation and the omission of the names of firms and individuals. The reason why only a small number of my reports are published is because the bulk of them were on business and economic subjects which would interest only a very few readers. The original copies of all these reports were sent to the Bureau of Foreign and Domestic Commerce in Washington and are still on file there.

Some people may wonder whether it is relevant to print now the text of reports written several years ago. One good answer is that ideas and impressions set down at the time are a better record than second guesses made long after the event. The material in this book shows how the Nazis appeared to me when they first seized power. This record also shows that while I always distrusted Nazi motives, I still, like most other observers, underestimated the Nazi capacity for evil. Hitler has seemed too bad to be true.

This material has all been submitted to the United States Department of Commerce and the Office of War Information in Washington, D. C., for checking before publication.

DOUGLAS MILLER

The following three reports, prepared before the Nazis got into power, show indications of what was coming in Germany. They also illustrate the difficulty that persons right on the spot had in interpreting the flow of events. These three reports do not present a consistent picture of Nazi intentions. Quite naturally they reflect the inconsistencies of the Nazi mind. The first one, entitled "National Socialism vs. American Business," was prepared on the basis of a long conversation with Hermann Goering. The second, "Economic Program of the National Socialists," came from another Nazi circle around Gregor Strasser and reports Nazi left-wing opinion. The third, on "Autarchy," reflects opinions expressed by the parlor Nazis, particularly those associated with the magazine called Die Tat *published in Dresden. Looking back, it is easy to compare these different types of programs and to see wherein they vary from each other; while at the time it was less easy to prophesy how seriously each type of Nazi program must be taken. . . .*

VIA DIPLOMATIC POUCH

I

NATIONAL SOCIALISM *vs.*
AMERICAN BUSINESS

Berlin, November 11, 1931

IT SEEMS INCREASINGLY LIKELY that the National Socialist party headed by Adolf Hitler will sooner or later be admitted to the German government. That government has since the war always been comprised of a coalition of various parties and undoubtedly if the National Socialists come into power it will be in a coalition with other groups, probably the Nationalists under Hugenberg, who stand for a return to pre-war conditions; the People's party, a party of large business enterprises and protective tariffs, and others. The National Socialists in the election on September 14, 1930, obtained a popular vote of over six million and were the second strongest party in the country. Municipal and provincial elections held since that date have shown increasing gains by the National Socialists. They claim now a popular vote of twelve million, which is not very far from the truth. If an election were held today they would indisputably be the strongest

13

party by far in Germany and could hardly be denied admission into the government. In any future election they are sure to poll a heavy vote, provided the business situation does not emphatically change for the better and the foreign relations of Germany are not smoothed out to the satisfaction of local pride. All the distress and discomfort of the present business depression have played into the hands of the National Socialists and they are growing rather than declining.

Next spring there is to be an election of the Prussian Diet which the present coalition government cannot postpone any longer. There will also be the election of a President to succeed Hindenburg. The National Socialists are certainly going to be a strong factor in both of these elections. If they succeed in capturing Prussia they can make things so uncomfortable for the federal government as practically to compel their admission into the coalition governing all of Germany or force a new election which would give them the power. All these considerations show that we must reckon with National Socialist participation in the German government, probably within a year.

What Is the National Socialist Party?

The National Socialists are not only the most numerous, but the best organized political group in Germany. They have understood how to attract support through the use of catchy slogans—"Freedom and Bread," "Germany Awake"—the wearing of a special uniform, the adoption of the Fascist salute, the use of marching songs and other things which appeal to the public. The party's central organization possesses a card-index system of its enrolled members, who pay a small monthly subscription and even pay small entrance fees into the numerous public assemblies which are held. The party possesses plenty of money raised in this way, or through the circulation of newspapers and periodicals, the sale of books and pamphlets and more recently even through the manufacture of cigarettes and other articles. The party also has a large war chest containing contributions from individuals and firms, running into very heavy sums. This money has been contributed partly by German industry in the belief that National Socialism offers an antidote to communism; and partly it has been subscribed by patriotically motivated people who desire the German government to adopt a stronger and more resistant attitude toward the French and other former enemies of Germany.

The National Socialists have never participated in the government and so have no responsibility for any of the government's acts to date. Thus they have a free hand to make the most sweeping criticisms of the present situation and to claim that the present government is responsible for all the ills and distress of the German people, which are very great and which arise, of course, from the loss of the war and the profound business depression now continuing. Every passing year takes the German public further from the days of the war and develops a generation of young Germans who naturally feel that they are unfairly penalized by events over which they had no control. They are anxious to break away from the Treaty of Versailles and all the results of the war, and every effort of the French and others to obtain reparation payments is good campaign material for the National Socialists.

The party also has a far-reaching economic policy which promises not only freedom from foreign domination, but a guaranteed livelihood for every German: "Freedom and Bread" are the watchwords. The party agrees with the communists that the present economic system is entirely false and that a new system must be erected. This apparently is to be something like communism but strongly German, with no foreign affiliation. On the one hand, the responsible leaders of the party have apparently assured many German industrialists that this program does not mean any injury to German industry and trade and is, in any event, better than socialism or communism; but the more rabid adherents of Hitler, on the other hand, are promising their followers a complete social and economic revolution, the extent of which can be judged by the resolution which the party introduced into the Reichstag shortly after the last election. This demanded an immediate nationalization of the banks and all large enterprises.

In addition to these basic proposals, the National Socialists have advocated, from time to time, the prohibition of department and chain stores, the reduction of the rate of interest by law to a maximum of five per cent, nationalization of the land or at any rate prohibition of land-ownership by foreigners and Jews and the division of large estates into smaller units, non-payment of foreign obligations, in particular those arising out of the war, compulsory enrollment of all able-bodied Germans into forced-labor organizations which shall insure everybody a job and a guaranteed wage. Some advocate the expulsion of Jews and foreigners from Germany, others propose that the State take over one-third of the ownership of all business enterprises, large or small, giving another one-third to the present owners and one-third to the workers. The government's one-third would take the place of taxation, since it is assumed that the profits thus derived would make other taxes unnecessary. The party also advocates national self-sufficiency in everything; some spokesmen come out for a foreign trade monopoly, closing the frontiers to passenger traffic and goods except in special cases, the development of Germany through its own resources and the elimination of foreign products. It is even stated by some persons that the country could learn to go without such foreign luxuries as coffee and tea and consume only true German commodities.

Economic "Program"

The above economic programs, however, are not clearly thought out and many of them are contradictory. It is apparent that the party has been attempting to get votes in every way and has put forward suggestions which might appeal to every class of voter in the country. Naturally, if and when the party gets into power, the greater part of these suggestions will be promptly forgotten and buried. It may be assumed that responsibility will sober the leaders; and that on the whole, after a certain amount of shake-up and turmoil, the German government would function very much as it does now and the economic system show very few changes.

None of the suggestions appears to have been well thought out; they are, in fact, not very strongly emphasized by most of the party leaders except when intended to define more clearly what is meant by "Freedom and Bread." In general, the party contents itself with slogans and marching displays, and leaves to the future the question of what they stand for. There are, however, a number of practical consequences to the National Socialist victory and inclusion in the government; and these must be faced, particularly as they may affect American business in Germany.

Practical Consequences for American Business

It is certain that a National Socialist government would take a rather hostile attitude toward foreign products and foreign firms engaged in business in this country. While no foreign trade monopoly or general import prohibition may be expected, there would undoubtedly be high tariffs and probably a series of import prohibitions of specific articles. The most dangerous measures to be expected, however, are internal regulations regarding the operation of business. One of the most sinister aspects of the situation is the payment of large sums to the party by particular German firms, who expect to get something in return. It is, for example, believed in the film industry and openly stated in the trade press that one of the German film companies, the Emelka in Munich, has a special understanding with the "Nazis," as they are called for short, that the Government would take a very strong line against the importation and exhibition of foreign pictures, particularly those pictures whose subject matter or treatment is not in accord with National Socialist beliefs.

An example of what might happen is shown by the street demonstrations against *All Quiet on the Western Front,* as a result of which the film was banned by the censor for some months in order to prevent trouble. It is probable that all films made by companies who have at any time offended the sensibilities of the Nazis will be barred from Germany. The Nazis are also opposed to jazz music, which they consider a barbarizing influence and which some people assert is part of a plot against the white race, or—as one of their leaders expressed it—an attempt to "niggerize" Germany.

It is believed in automotive circles that some of the German automotive manufacturers have given the Nazis money with the understanding that special legislation should be directed against the Opel Company, which is eighty per cent owned by an American firm. Opel has been producing recently a small cheap car which has had a remarkable success, and its competitors would like to curtail this business through political means.

Another example of the type of legislation which may be expected is the proposed legislation against department and chain stores now being brought forward in Wuerttemberg. This would restrict their activities in many cases; and it provides that in places of less than twenty thousand inhabitants these stores shall not be allowed to exist unless the local magistrates are convinced of the necessity.

The Nazis would also probably get after American advertising agencies here and the firms employing them, since they consider advertising slogans such as are in common use in America to be unfair competition. Many of the business-getting devices practiced by American companies, too, they regard as unfair competition. This includes the giving away of free samples or the use of statements regarding the competitive quality of the product.

Nazis are hostile to all foreigners and foreign influence, but in particular they have singled out the Jews for their greatest animosity. Street demonstrations in which Jews and persons looking like them have been killed or severely beaten are very common occurrences. Examples are the riot which occurred in Berlin on last September 12, the Jewish New Year, or the demonstration following the opening of the Reichstag in October, 1930, when windows of Jewish stores were broken all over the business district.

2

ECONOMIC PROGRAM OF THE
NATIONAL SOCIALISTS

Berlin, August 23, 1932

THE ECONOMIC SECTION of the National Socialist party has prepared a pamphlet, edited by Gregor Strasser, which is the official textbook of the party's "immediate" economic program. All National Socialist speakers are warned against any departure from the principles therein laid down.

In general, it is made clear, the National Socialist economic program involves cutting off the country from the rest of the world by means of a foreign trade monopoly; by an official control of foreign exchange, with the necessary prohibitions in regard to trading in foreign exchange by private persons, which is punishable by the death penalty; by the turning over of the banks and large industries to government ownership and the undertaking of an immense plan for improving the country's economic structure. The emphasis is laid on improving agricultural production, which is to be raised from the present figure to one hundred per cent of the nation's consumption.

At the same time, workmen are to be colonized in their own homes on the land, each in his own garden, thus taking them away from the large cities, first in order to increase the food supply by gardening, secondly to improve the conditions of health and work and, thirdly, to reduce the danger of foreign bombing and gas attacks.

The financing of this scheme is to be done by the government, but it is promised that no inflation will result, because of the reduced taxes made possible by the stoppage of reparations and unemployment doles. However, a maximum income of 500 marks per month, about $120, is taken as a limit for public employees and this is in general not to be much exceeded in private business, although some allowance is to be made for the fact that in certain cases there is insecurity of employment and no provision for old age pensions. It is calculated that agricultural improvements, such as draining swamps, will cost about ten billion marks and will bring in two billion marks per year in the form of increased production.

Foreign goods are to be kept out of Germany by import restrictions whenever they can be duplicated inside the country. The necessary raw materials and, in the beginning, certain foodstuffs are to be allowed to come in from those countries which are particular friends and co-operators of the National Socialists in Germany, but in no case is more to be allowed to come in from any country than Germany exports in return. The German long-term foreign indebtedness is to have its rate of interest reduced to the level of interest in the creditor country. An agreement is to be made with the short-term creditors for a postponement of their claims for several years. The foreign-exchange restrictions are to be made airtight and to cover even the smallest amounts of money and to be retroactive to include all existing transactions. There is to be a most severe control of all foreign undertakings in Germany and all German undertakings abroad to prevent evasion of the foreign-exchange laws, an offense punishable by death.

The gold standard is to be abandoned. All banks are to be placed under ownership of the government. The use of checks is to be encouraged and postal checks are to be made of a size to be carried in the pocket. The domestic rate of interest is to be reduced. Prices are to be controlled by the government. All extravagance in public and private life is to disappear. Special taxes are to be laid on all incomes of over 500 marks per month, and additional taxes on all incomes of over 15,000 marks per year. Public officials may in no case receive more than 1,000 marks per month: in private business the rate is but little more. New factories and machine installations are to be prohibited, unless they are necessary to substitute for present imported goods. The entire organization of department stores and chain stores is to be revised with the idea of protecting the small retailer and the consumer. German workmen and German material are to be given preference to foreign. Social insurance is to be maintained. Compulsory physical labor for all young Germans is to be set up, not to combat unemployment, but to train the youth in physical labor, bind together all classes of the population and increase respect for manual work.

3

AUTARCHY

Berlin, December 12, 1932

THE WORD AUTARCHY in the sense of economic self-sufficiency has been in everybody's mouth, at least in Germany, during the last year. Its sponsors are for the most part from the younger generation and closely allied to the National Socialist movement. The principles and the practice of autarchy have recently been outlined in a book by Ferdinand Fried, the pen name of one of the thoroughgoing supporters of this idea and probably its most prominent exponent.

Autarchy as outlined by Fried seems to have little touch with present economic realities. It is a dream and a bad dream at that. Fried pictures Germany entirely cut off economically from the rest of the world except for a small amount of barter, which would be principally directed toward Germany's south-eastern neighbors in the exchange of a small amount of finished products for certain raw material imports.

This would probably create a country in which very few

people would care to live, but the adherents of this idea believe that the principles of freedom of trade have been shown to be unsound and to end in a world-wide economic depression with consequent unemployment. They propose a return to semi-medieval conditions whereby the large cities are to be deserted, with almost everyone settling upon the land where each can do his own little gardening and where needs are reduced to the simplest. The individual shall no longer be left free to choose his own vocation; and the principle of authority and a definite class system shall be made prominent. Autarchy is to be inaugurated by severing all financial ties with the outside world, and by complete repudiation of public and private indebtedness. The future internal currency shall be based upon the credit of the country and have no connection with foreign currencies or gold.

It looks to a skeptic as if the advocates of this idea are young idealists who are profoundly dissatisfied with post-war Germany's political and economic position in the world, and therefore think it better not to play the game any more according to the old rules, but to go off in a corner and play by themselves, making up their own rules as they go along.

These idealists believe that they can discern a universal discontent with present-day liberalism, materialism and nationalism. They believe that people are ripe for a return to the simple life of medieval times, sacrificing material comforts for the sake of greater emphasis on their own tradition and their national and racial peculiarities. They are perfectly aware that a general repudiation of debts and a refusal to buy foreign goods would be equivalent to a blockade of Germany's frontiers; they believe that in times of peace, with all national efforts concentrated on the production of foodstuffs and necessary raw materials, the country could get along without foreigners. A detailed consideration of specific commodities shows the extent to which they believe that this is possible.

Imports of all kinds of grain and of animal fodders are unnecessary since the greater use of rye and potatoes can provide enough food of this kind for man and beast in Germany. This statement may be correct as far as the year 1932 is concerned, which was characterized by a splendid crop, but these hopes are subject to a considerable uncertainty if future crops do not always come up to this high level. Germany is far more than self-supporting in potatoes and, under autarchy, she could use some of the land now devoted to potatoes for other foodstuffs. Furthermore, potatoes can be used to produce alcohol as a substitute for imported gasoline, and dried potato flakes can be used for animal fodder instead of barley.

In fresh meats Germany is now ninety-nine per cent self-supporting and can get along without foreign imports.

As far as milk, butter, cheese and eggs are concerned, the local production can be raised to make up for the loss of imports by using land now devoted to potatoes.

In sugar Germany has an export surplus, and at least two hundred fifty thousand acres now used for sugar beets can be made free for growing other types of foodstuffs.

In fresh vegetables and fruits, foreign imports are not so much a matter of necessity as of luxury. German farmers can supply the demand throughout the year, if the public is willing to accept a uniform diet of the vegetables which will keep over the winter, such as cabbage, turnips, cauliflower, carrots, and beets. Fresh vegetables all the year round are a luxury which it is believed the German public should not try to afford. Large sums of money are spent annually for early potatoes, early peas and other out-of-season products which are primarily a luxury. The same is true of fruit. The author complains that German gardeners sell their apples in the fall at low prices, whereas the Americans hold back from the market until the winter when the price is high and in this way obtain an unfair advantage. He believes that with better marketing methods, German fruit can satisfy the market, and that the public can give up without any severe loss its present taste for bananas, oranges and overseas apples which, by the way, he says, look better and taste worse than the domestic fruit.

As far as fish is concerned, it is evident that Germany can increase its own fisheries by adding three hundred new ships to its fishing fleet, thus stopping the necessity of imports from foreign fisheries.

Tea, coffee, chocolate are considered as unnecessary stimulants which can well be dispensed with, actually improving the health of the population thereby, or as the author says: "Shall we drink coffee just to please Brazil or drink coffee so that we can continue selling machines or buttons?"

With regard to tobacco, the author believes that German tobacco could satisfy all demands, but fails to realize that the only varieties which Germany has been growing up to the present time are those suitable for pipe and chewing tobacco and not suitable for cigarettes.

As far as foreign fats are concerned, Germany will need imports of certain fats, such as palm oil, but can cut down the amount necessary by increasing the sowings of soya beans.

In textile raw materials, Germany can increase its wool, flax and hemp production and will need far less cotton if its cotton industry does not have to produce for export.

In lumber, certain foreign imports of special hardwoods and paper for pulp will be necessary, although imports of hides, skins and furs will be practically unnecessary.

The import of ores from abroad will be unnecessary since the iron and steel industry can get along by using German ores and scrap. Imported copper can be replaced by domestic aluminum.

Germany has enough supplies of domestic coal and brown coal and can substitute alcohol and synthetic petroleum for imported petroleum and gasoline. The loss of imported phosphates can be made up by using more Thomas meal. Naval stores can be made synthetically.

A certain amount of mercury, sulphur, platinum, etc., must necessarily be imported, but can be paid for in finished goods. No foreign finished goods are to be imported, as German industries can be considered competent to produce everything needed by the population. On the other hand, foreign countries can easily be found which can absorb the German exports of finished goods totaling 2.4 billions of marks yearly. The author points out that even in the depression year 1931, Russia and Central Europe took 1.6 billions of finished goods. This is to be the future field for finished goods for German industry, which is to have not only an economic but a political orientation toward the east and the southeast of Europe. The author estimates that at the present time there are not more than 1.6 million workers who are employed on goods for export. These persons can be set doing useful work to improve Germany's interior situation.

Autarchy is to free Germany from her present foreign indebtedness, from dependence on foreign banks, insurance companies and shipping and, by uniting Eastern and Central Europe in an economic entity, create a portion of the world in which German interests will be dominant and Germany will have future room for expansion. Germany is to turn her back upon the West, just as Great Britain in the Ottawa Conference has turned away from the other countries toward her own dominions and as other countries, including the United States, have become more self-contained by protective tariffs, import contingents and foreign-exchange restrictions.

After the Nazis assumed power in 1933, they began an energetic campaign to control and police all organs influencing public opinion, and thus they made sure of retaining their hold on the situation. The first few months of Nazi administration were thus largely devoted to securing themselves from attack from other parties in Germany. By the early summer of 1933 the National Socialist party was so entrenched that its leaders could begin more ambitious programs and actually put into practice the ideas they had been germinating for more than ten years. The following thirteen reports, prepared and submitted in 1933 and early 1934, reflect the situation as it developed from day to day and give a better flavor of the early days of Nazism than can be obtained in other ways. Of course these reports contain many errors in judgment; in particular they failed to assess the growing importance of military considerations in the Nazi mind. This mistake is quite logical because the German military machine was operating in the dark, while the political and economic programs dominated the spotlight. . . .

4

"GLEICHSCHALTUNG"

Berlin, May 3, 1933

On May first, Chancellor Hitler publicly announced his economic program for the first year of the National Socialist régime. Characteristically, the main points of the program are not economic but political. He laid special emphasis on the necessity for national unity, recovery of German self-esteem, stoppage of class warfare and strengthening of the national will to improve Germany's position in the world. The definite economic points of the program are as follows:

Organization, this year, of compulsory labor battalions for all young Germans; it is planned that every German youth must spend some period of time in manual labor, probably with only nominal pay and under semi-military discipline. The expenditure of some billions of marks upon a program of public works. Hitler mentions specifically the building of roads and the erection and improvement of buildings, the encouragement of and the insistence upon private expenditure to create employment.

All these points are simply the continuation of the program which not only this government but preceding cabinets have followed. There is practically nothing new except the announcement that a general compulsory labor battalion will be started this year. The essence of the government's economic program is not to be found so much in public statements as in an examination of the acts of the government since taking office. These indicate enough so that a careful observer can already begin to draw definite conclusions regarding the way in which things are going.

The most important policy of the government is to obtain complete control of all phases of activity in Germany. This has already been pretty well accomplished. Every organization for whatever purpose, every activity in which Germans are engaged, is being put in line with the National Socialist policy. This is called *Gleichschaltung*.

The most recent example occurred yesterday when Nazi followers took over the headquarters of the trade unions known as *Allgemeiner Deutscher Gewerkschaftsbund*, arrested sixty of the leading officials and practically forced the trade unions to become an integral part of the Nazi organization. It is only a week since the seven hundred thousand war veterans of the *Stahlhelm* were told they must either enter the National Socialist party or resign membership in the *Stahlhelm*. Organizations such as trade unions, trade associations, religious, educational, artistic or sport societies have practically all been put in line, quite irrespective of what type of activity they represent, as for example the Society of Church Organists, the Berlin Chess Players, the Amateur and Professional Boxers and the *Reichsverband der deutschen Industrie*.

There is to be in Germany only one will and that is the will of the leader of the National Socialist party, only one plan and that is the National Socialist program. Every business organization now must have its Nazi cell which supervises everything that goes on and reports to the National Socialist party any items of interest or importance. This is making it increasingly difficult for foreign firms to operate here, and is bearing out the program which was reported by this office about one and a half years ago, namely that foreign enterprises in Germany will be so severely restricted by the National Socialist régime that they must become German or eventually get out. The general cause of contention between foreign enterprises here and the National Socialists is the insistence of the latter that expenditures must be maintained or increased and that persons must not be discharged or business restricted. This puts foreign companies which are running at a loss here into a difficult position. They must either continue to run at an increasing loss or face the possibility of losing whatever investments they have inside Germany. It is certainly advisable for American firms to refrain from making new investments in Germany at the present time. As long as American firms keep their investments outside of Germany and merely try to sell to Germans, their position is much stronger.

After the Nazis have achieved their purpose of obtaining complete control of every activity in Germany, the next step is the unification and centralization of authority, already illustrated by the practical disappearance of the states and provinces and a series of uniform regulations which are now being issued daily. A vast machine with highly centralized control is coming into being. This machine is a double one; one half of it is the official structure and the other the purely party organization; both operate in unison, as they are linked together not only at the top in the person of Hitler, who is leader in the party and in the government, but all the way down the line where in each little village the local leader of the Nazi party is in close touch with the local officials and dignitaries, who, of course, are also Nazis or soon will be.

One aspect of the Nazi tactics is the excellent advertising and stage management of the whole show. Everything the party does must be the biggest of its kind. Hitler, Goering and Goebbels are constantly pounding the big drum, playing to the gallery. Probably their future actions will also be colored by this tendency, even in the economic field.

It is interesting to speculate over what the National Socialist employment program will look like. Hitler already announces that billions will be spent. Certainly no money can be borrowed from abroad, nor can taxes be raised very considerably in Germany. Therefore, the only apparent source of revenue for the compulsory labor battalions, the program of public works, etc., must come from some kind of credit inflation inside Germany, either by advances from the Reichsbank which will be practicable for moderate amounts or an issue of government bonds. In this latter case, it seems likely that the banks and large companies would be practically forced to take prescribed quotas. It is not likely that the general public would be directly asked to subscribe very much, for the government would hardly wish to risk a failure. If this course of credit inflation is pursued it will put renewed pressure on the government to revalue the mark, especially after the pound and dollar become stabilized at lower levels. The balance of opinion points to some action of this kind in the course of the present year. The only alternative would be to tighten existing financial and foreign-exchange restrictions, sacrifice what is left of German export trade and separate more widely than at present the artificial exchange value of the mark abroad from its domestic purchasing value inside Germany, which is sure to go down if the government's plans are put into effect.

Before any change occurs in the value of the mark, the first thing to be got out of the way is the transfer problem. Informed persons in Germany now expect some sort of transfer moratorium at an early date, with the probability that foreign creditors will be asked to take interest payments in blocked marks. Americans will be generally well advised to keep their capital out of Germany at the present and to go slow on new commitments. The sales campaigns of American companies here are being handicapped not so much by any definite action on the part of the government as by the spontaneous and universal feeling in Germany that all foreign persons, products and even ideas are somewhat under suspicion until they have been officially pronounced as suitable by the Nazis.

Thus American film companies now are complaining that theater owners are canceling contracts for American pictures, on the grounds that they are not suitable for the new Germany. American automobile companies state that potential customers are afraid to buy foreign cars not because the government has said anything about it, but because their neighbors may believe they are lukewarm in national spirit. There is certainly a very strong wave of nationalistic feeling going over the country, and everybody desires to avoid being associated with anything foreign. It is even noticed that our German friends and acquaintances of long standing are much more reserved and do not see us nearly so often as formerly. People are much less free to talk, they lower their voices in the presence of strangers and look round to see who is listening. This is more marked in the small towns than in Berlin.

Among the most worried are the German Nationalists, who feel deeply the desertion of the *Stahlhelm* leaders and are wondering just how much longer Hugenberg, Neurath and Schwerin-Krosigk can hold on to their jobs. There is a growing feeling here that the Nationalist influence in the cabinet will soon be reduced to a purely nominal one. It is even suggested that Hitler may prefer to call in new allies from the *Zentrum* who will be more in sympathy with his economic program than the Nationalists, who were only useful to him at the start.

5

THE "ORGANIC SOCIETY"

Berlin, May 10, 1933

As SUGGESTED in our previous reports, the National Socialist movement is busy framing the outline of a new form of economic organization which is to arise in Germany. They are thoroughgoing believers in the organic state or the organic society—that is to say, Germany is to be regarded as a definite living entity whose welfare and growth are of absolute and supreme importance. The duty of each individual German is to this society, and the welfare of the whole is more important than the welfare of the individual. It is the duty of each person to subordinate his welfare to that of the group, giving his property, his time and even his life, if necessary. There is no distinction in this between times of peace and war. An individual exists for the State and not the State for the individual; this theory is a very old one in Germany.

On the economic side this organic structure is to be built up on what the Nazis call *Staende*, or estates; there is no good English equivalent for that phrase since we do not have the same conception. It has not yet been decided how many *Staende*

37

there shall be. Two have already been definitely organized, namely trade and handicrafts. Others to follow are agriculture, the professions, industry and labor, although some authorities say that industry and labor will be only one estate. It is not yet known whether these estates will be organized together in some super-organization or whether the existing *Reichswirtschafts-rat* may provide a representation for them all. The estates are to include and supplement existing economic organizations such as trade unions, employers' associations, cartels, etc. Cartels as such are not entirely to disappear, but will become official instead of unofficial and all firms in the trade must belong to them.

Emphasis will be put on retaining all existing plants whether or not they are economically justified. All firms which are now existing will be kept going if possible. The idea is to prevent persons from losing their jobs. Weaker firms are to be protected and supported. Stronger firms and those earning undue profits will be closely watched and are likely to have their wings clipped. In given trades where profits are small no new competitors are to be allowed; this is illustrated by a six-months' prohibition just issued against the erection of any more retail shops in Germany. Retailers in particular are to be protected by a gradual elimination of their competitors, the consumers' co-operatives, which are damned because of their long connection with the Social Democrats, and the department and chain stores, which have a strong Jewish flavor and are not politically as important as the great body of retailers.

The department stores are to be reduced in their scope. They must, first of all, erect no new branches, they must give up any manufacturing enterprises which they possess and they must gradually cut down a number of their departments; the greatest eyesore in the view of the Nazis being the grocery departments, followed by the restaurants and refreshment rooms.

It is planned to reduce the department stores, finally, to large shops handling either clothing or furniture, or perhaps, as a great concession, both of these lines.

This information is obtained from statements made by the new chiefs of the "estate for trade." What the plan of the other estates will be, is yet unknown, but there is a great deal of conjecture and some indication from past utterances of important Nazis. The chief principle of the permanent status of the individual is to be emphasized. In other words, each person is born or otherwise called into a certain place in German society; he is expected to fill that place to the best of his ability, to serve the State loyally and to stay put. The individual will not decide very much of anything for himself; everything will be decided for him. He is to live frugally, modestly, and contribute cheerfully to the welfare of the whole. The coming generations are to be schooled to take their places in this form of society. The first real introduction to their lifework will be the compulsory year of manual labor which each German youth must undergo when he is nineteen. This is to commence on January first, next, when three hundred and fifty thousand boys of nineteen will be called for service. The first two groups will work only six months each; but beginning in the January of 1935, each group will work a complete year. It is planned at first to employ them largely on improving the land. There is claimed to be work ahead for eight or nine years. Each boy will be furnished with a uniform and other clothing, will be fed and sheltered at the State's expense. The boys will spend six hours of each work-day in productive work and three hours in drill and exercises. No doubt most of them will be turned out as thoroughly standardized young Nazis and will willingly and obediently take their places in the particular estates to which accident of birth or a decision of the party may assign them.

It is hard for Americans to take this sort of thing seriously, but it is actually being put into operation and apparently has a long run ahead of it. Where the Nazis got their ideas is not hard to fathom. Some of them are borrowed from the Fascisti, others from the Soviets. There is just a suggestion of guild socialism about the *Staende* and a strong medieval flavor to the whole plan.

The Nazis as a whole are young, ignorant and romantic; most of them have never had any material success in the modern capitalistic world and they are quite ready to declare it a failure and vote for a return to a medieval status where the individual does not have to do his own thinking. This Nazi revolution was after all accomplished by a few fanatics and adventurers who had learned how to appeal to the moron majority in a period of depression and discouragement.

This campaign for popular support has been successful and the German people of their own choice have given the Nazi leaders complete authority over them for years in advance. Here is probably one of the greatest examples of mass stupidity ever seen in modern times. The public has not yet realized what it has done, but it will soon begin to pay the bill in voluntary contributions, forced loans, high taxes and possibly even in war. At any rate it has certainly got to feed an army of about one million Storm Troopers and Elite Guards and other Nazi functionaries who are now the heroes of the national revolution and expect to be supported in easy jobs by the rest of the country from now on.

Wealthy people who originally supported the Nazis as a bulwark against bolshevism are only now beginning to see that they have been fixing the yoke of their saviors around their necks for an indefinite period. German business has got to pay the bill principally in the forthcoming series of forced loans—but, even before that, in voluntary contributions. The

Nazis already are frying the fat out of everybody who has any money; so-called voluntary contributions for the upkeep of Storm Troopers and Elite Guards are the order of the day. This is all done in the name of the sacredness of private property and abhorrence of bolshevik tactics, but it does not sound very orthodox to German capitalists.

It is practically impossible now for any firm to dismiss an employee who has any contact with the Nazis. A few days ago the Eden Hotel dismissed two employees. These complained to the Nazi cell in the hotel, which took the matter up with the management. The management showed that the hotel was losing money, but the chief of the cell, after examining the books, found that the hotel was paying seven per cent interest on a loan. The matter was taken up with the Nazi party and the bank which had advanced the money was forced to reduce the rate to four per cent. This gave the two employees their jobs back and may temporarily have pleased the hotel management, but, of course, from now on the Nazi cell is the boss.

In the Adlon Hotel a Nazi *Kommissar* has been appointed who lives the life of Riley and who has to be consulted by the manager on every decision.

The head of an insurance company told me yesterday that they had been shaken down for fifty thousand marks for the S.A. Otherwise, they would have had to go out of business.

There is no need to multiply these examples. Any important German company could tell you the same story if they only dared. The big fellows are certainly being bled in a thousand ways at the same time. This shows that the Nazis can play practical politics with the best. Whether they will be satisfied with this form of graft or whether the proletarian elements of the party will insist on further sweeping measures, is not yet clear, but probably the latter is the size of it. A taste of power and easy money is likely only to whet the appetites of these heroes.

6

THE "ESTATES"

Berlin, May 12, 1933

As MENTIONED IN PREVIOUS REPORTS, the National Socialist plan for organizing and operating the economic life of Germany divides the country along occupational lines. A number of *Staende,* or estates, are now in process of organization, representing all persons, firms or organizations having to do with trade, handicrafts, agriculture, professions, industry, and labor. The relation of the individual to the nation will be for the most part an indirect one. The individual in the future is to have much less freedom of choice and activity, and will only to a limited extent be able to deal directly with the state or public bodies—in, for example, the making of contracts, operations on the stock market, banking and insurance transactions, carrying on processes before the courts, and similar matters. The greater part of his relations to other people and the public in general will be conducted through his occupational group, which will take group instead of individual action.

In each locality all members of a given group will be organized in a local body (*Bezirksorganisation*). These, in turn, will be part of a larger group (*Kreisorganisation*) which, in turn, forms part of the provincial group and finally the national organization. For example, all employers, workmen and associates of the metal trade in each district will be organized together and form part of the chain which links them to the national organization. Employers and employees will be grouped together, thus practically cutting the ground from under the feet of existing trade unions, trade associations and similar bodies. The officials and leaders of various groups are not to be elected by popular votes, but are to be chosen by the existing leaders on the basis of their experience and ability. The principle of popular vote and majority rule is discarded in favor of the principle of leadership and authority. The national organizations will then comprise the leaders representing various local and provincial groups and will, in turn, form part of the national estate. This national estate will comprise roughly one hundred and fifty to two hundred persons.

The functions of the estate and its component bodies are very large in scope. Firstly, legislative: making the rules and regulations which are to govern all persons within their organization. Secondly, the estate will have executive functions; it will have the right to determine its own membership, to control the daily life of its members, to define and maintain the rights and privileges of each. Furthermore, the estate will have judicial functions, deciding the rights and wrongs of complaints and passing on claims and controversies. It will have very large powers of arbitration in disputed cases. The estate itself is not so much a parliamentary body as an organization of committees of officials and will function mainly in committee. Nevertheless, the estates are not a final source of authority, but are to be subordinate to the national government.

Each estate will have the right to set conditions, terms and standards within its own field. For the most part each estate will determine the hours of labor, wages and salary rates, prices, production quotas, standards of quality, units of measurement, patent rights and—one very important item—the power to limit or fix the number of participants in any given group. The *Numerus Clausus*, or fixed number of participants in any given group, which principle has already been adopted for lawyers, doctors and students in the universities, will be generally adopted. Every attempt will be made to protect and retain existing firms and individuals in the exercise of their present trades and careful scrutiny will be given to all persons who desire to enter the ranks. The estates will also have considerable power of recommendation regarding taxation of their own branch, naturally in consultation with the national government.

The estates will have almost complete control of vocational education, admission of apprentices and students. They will devote themselves to improving the social conditions in their field, organizing sports for workers and supervising the free time of their members. Each person in their ranks will be encouraged to keep busy in his free hours, attending meetings, marching in parades, listening to exhortations, planting gardens, playing tennis, football and other sports under proper control, all to the glory of the particular occupation and of the German people.

The estates will, of course, be subject to the control of the national government at the very top, but all the way down they will be linked closely to government officials in each district and to the local organization of the National Socialist party. In each town, city or village the government officials will work closely with the party officials and the estate officials. Great difficulties can be foreseen in the clash of interests between one estate and another. There is certainly much to be said for the principle of organizing employers and employees in any given branch of trade or industry for the common good of the trade. The trouble is that the most solid basis of such organizations is the determination to press the interests of the particular trade as against the interests of the general public and other trades. In this way the government will have to be the final arbitrator or umpire among the conflicting interests of the different estates; for example: it can be readily seen that all persons connected with agriculture and organized in the agricultural estate will have the greatest interest in high prices for agricultural products, coupled with protection against foreign imports, and a desire to utilize all available resources of German soil regardless of whether this is economically profitable or not. The other estates will, on the contrary, have a direct interest in keeping food prices low. The national government will certainly have its hands full in reconciling such a conflict of interests.

The above program amounts to nothing less than a complete reorganization of all branches of economic life with the control placed in the hands of individuals who will obtain recognition for their services to the National Socialist party. True enough, many of these people are no doubt honest and able, but their experience in organizing a revolutionary political campaign does not particularly fit them to have the final say in all the intricate matters of business. Furthermore, the majority of the new crowd are people of little means and little experience in handling money. In economic matters their sympathies are decidedly toward the "left"; along with their strong "right" idea in national military questions, there has been a decided swing toward the political "left" in the National Socialist party since it came into office. Germany is essentially a proletarian country and any popular movement here must take this into consideration. In fact, this explains the extreme bitterness of the Nazis toward Social Democratic and communist leaders who were their competitors in attracting the sympathies of the masses. The Nazis could far more easily tolerate upper-class minorities, because they knew that their support would always be confined to a small group.

Wealthy Germans are only now opening their eyes to the essential radicalism of the Nazi government. It is bound to be more radical than Italian Fascism. In the last few days we have received many reports of the greatest uneasiness and anxiety among German business leaders. Only too gladly would they leave the country if they could take their property along. For the most part they will have to stay and stick it out, giving full support to the new government in spite of their skepticism and anxiety, because they feel it is not possible to go back now and that a failure of the Nazi movement would leave the communists the best chance of getting power. Certainly the masses, if completely disillusioned by the Nazi movement, might turn to communism as their last hope. For this reason, practically all Germans are going to pull together in support of the present movement. The Germans as a people, with their qualities of discipline, order, industry, and gullibility, make admirable material for the new form of organization. They are more likely to make a success of it than any other people similarly placed; in spite of the crudity which the new movement is showing, it seems likely that it will not break down from any internal difficulties. The chief obstacle will be found in the foreign political situation.

7

GROWING RADICALISM

Berlin, May 19, 1933

As the National Socialist government comes to closer grips with the realities of the present situation, it still continues to represent almost unanimous German opinion on questions of disarmament, treaty revision and military affairs in general, but in the economic field it is drifting further from its former Nationalist colleagues. Although the movement was originally financed in large part by big industries, its chief support at the present time is found among the masses of the unemployed, the laborers and the white-collar employees who are struggling along on low wages. The National Socialist revolution is no longer to be called merely a national revolution, according to Dr. Goebbels in his speech last Sunday. It is not merely an assertion of Germany's rights against other nations, but a readjustment of class and occupational inequalities inside the country.

Voices in the country will not down, but keep referring to the former doctrine of the party that all incomes shall be limited;

for example, that no salaries shall be paid anywhere in Germany exceeding 12,000 marks, or roughly three thousand dollars per year. Persons of wealth and importance are suspect under the new régime. Commissioner Wagner, new head of the German Manufacturers' Association, has just made a public statement which illustrates the extent to which wealthy and prominent people have already been penalized and what they are likely to suffer in the future. Among other things he admits that a wave of denunciations against important persons in the country has been going on in the last few weeks, causing investigations and arrests for flight of capital, tax evasion and other crimes peculiar to wealthy men. In many cases this has not occurred through patriotic motives: envious and spiteful persons have been using the movement to cause trouble for their more fortunate fellow citizens. Commissioner Wagner goes on to say that this is unfortunate, for one reason, because in the financing of the forthcoming employment program, wealthy people are going to be called upon to subscribe heavily. He adds that it is their patriotic duty to subscribe, even if they are not personally of the opinion that the plans of the government are wise or likely to be successful.

One inducement which Commissioner Wagner proposes to stimulate subscriptions for internal loans is a general amnesty for past tax evasion and flight of capital, provided such funds are duly brought back and subscribed to the forthcoming loans; but, he adds, whoever allows this opportunity to pass by and places his own welfare before the public interest, will be suspected of treason to the country and the German people and may expect no mercy if caught in the meshes of the law. To put this more plainly: wealthy persons and, more particularly, Jews, are all more or less under suspicion, and they will be expected to contribute heavily to forthcoming loans. This may work out at something not very far removed from actual confiscation of property.

The radical character of the National Socialist movement may be more clearly shown when the new employment plans get fully under way. One section of the National Socialist party is already openly discussing the use of the one-year conscripted laborers, who will be called to work on January first, not only in improving agricultural lands, draining swamps, building roads, etc., but in factories producing goods for export. It is thought that a number of factories manufacturing staple merchandise, and which are in financial difficulties, may be allowed to go bankrupt or be condemned to be taken away from their former owners and manned by these nineteen-year-old boys who have one year of forced labor to perform for the Fatherland. The hours of labor would be short; two shifts of five or six hours each might possibly be employed, and the goods would be solely or principally devoted to the export market. It can be imagined what kind of a reception such goods would have in the United States and many other countries.

From day to day orders and decrees continue to appear in the press warning individuals against independent action and urging the maintenance of discipline. These orders result from the independent and spontaneous actions of individual Nazis, who take it upon themselves to interfere with other people's business, particularly with the operation of factories, shops and other commercial enterprises. Multitudes of such cases have already occurred. They are condemned in principle by the leaders of the party and government officials, but condoned in practice, if for no other reason than the fact that the Nazi chieftains, Hitler, Goering, Goebbels and the rest are simply too busy to check up on all the small actions that are going on. The newspapers and the radio have several times declared that these few well-known Nazis beg the public not to call upon them, telephone them, or write them, if it can possibly be avoided, as they are completely overwhelmed by the mass of complaints, claims, denunciations and requests which have already flooded their offices.

Most radical of all the Nazi organizations is the N.S.B.O., the *National Socialist Betriebszellen Organisation,* which has a cell in each place where people are employed. Two days ago over the radio an official of this group described how they had just transferred their headquarters to the building formerly occupied by the Metal Workers' Union. He pictured this building five stories high, furnished with leather chairs, conference tables, a marble staircase and similar luxuries paid for by the workmen's *pfennige,* and added that the new National Socialist officials were not planning to use the front door or the marble staircase, as their hobnailed boots would slip on the marble. They were planning to use only the back door and one floor of the building to house their modest necessities. Neither were they planning to use the washbowls which were lavishly supplied in different offices, as they had come into office with clean hands and in the future their hands would be blackened only by honest work and they would never be ashamed to grasp hands with the hornyhanded sons of toil. Furthermore, they would have neither time nor inclination to sit in the leather armchairs which were built for the portly figures of bloated trade-union executives of the corrupt Social Democratic days.

The *Frankfurter Zeitung* carries a story that the Director of Koenigsberg University, Dr. Preyer, has made a public speech regarding the necessity of maintaining the capitalist system and citing Hitler as defending this system. He was at once taken up by the local leader of the National Socialist *Studentenschaft,* who pointed out that the capitalist system is responsible for the ills of the present and that Hitler, by his public announcements and his actions since he obtained power, proves that he is making a clean break with the capitalistic past. The *Rektor* is warned not to refer to Hitler, in the future, as a believer in capitalism.

The Nationalist elements in the government grouped around Hugenberg are just now making their last desperate stand to maintain the influence of capital and particularly to maintain the large landowners against the onrushing wave of the National Socialist masses. Hugenberg has just published a statement in which he attempts to restrict the activities of the new Commissioner, Wagner, who has taken over the *Reichsverband der deutschen Industrie.*

Hugenberg has also come into sharp conflict with Darré, the head of the National Socialist agrarian group, regarding the question of interest rates on farm mortgages. He insists that the rate be maintained as high as four to four and one-half per cent, while the National Socialists demand that it shall be reduced to two and one-half per cent. The *Angriff,* local organ of the National Socialist party, is already discussing this stand of Hugenberg in threatening language. It does not seem likely that he can retain even the sharply restricted power which he now enjoys. Hugenberg's right-hand man, Under-Secretary Bang, has also come out in the papers with a plea for moderation in taking over existing industries. He warns the National Socialists against going too far in the direction of state socialism. It is probable that he also will lose his position or give in to the majority opinion.

There is, however, one factor which may delay the forced sinking of interest rates on mortgages and that is the necessity of floating new loans to finance the employment program. It is asking a good deal of German capitalists to subscribe to new issues at the same time that the interest rates on existing mortgage bonds are being so drastically cut.

8

CHANGES AND DECREES

Berlin, June 13, 1933

IN THE LAST TWO WEEKS the progress of the National Socialist movement in Germany has been marked by several important changes and decrees, most of which have already been reported by this office. These include a transfer moratorium, on the payment of interest on German obligations abroad, incurred before July, 1931, with the exception of those obligations covered by the Standstill Agreement, which provided for the temporary freezing of foreign credits in Germany; the series of decrees announcing a grant of one thousand marks to individual married couples, under certain conditions, with a compensating tax on bachelors; the program of emergency employment to be financed to the extent of one billion marks by what amounts to short-term borrowing from the Reichsbank, and the announcement of a national fund to which persons may contribute in a hope of future amnesty when detected in tax evasion or violation of foreign-exchange regulations.

As an illustration of National Socialist policy in provincial districts, it is reported that the party in the district of Cassel is planning a special emergency levy for the local relief of unemployment and the placing of children upon the land for the summer. The levy will run four months and is to be met as follows: five per cent of the wages of all persons employed in public enterprises, three marks per month for unmarried workers with from one hundred to one hundred and fifty marks monthly income, from three to eighteen per cent on higher incomes, one mark fifty from married workers earning up to one hundred and fifty marks per month, and from two to twelve per cent per month on higher incomes. In addition, firms are to pay certain fixed sums, and real-estate owners one-half per cent of the pre-war rent each month. According to court decisions in several parts of the country, failure in giving the Hitler greeting, that is, raising the right arm on public occasions, is to be regarded as an act disturbing the peace and punishable by imprisonment for several days. The official press bureau of the party has publicly announced that firms are requested to give special attention to National Socialist party members of long standing and that in particular all party members carrying membership cards numbered from 1 to 100,000 are to have preference in obtaining employment.

The Ministry of Posts has announced that, in the spelling of words over the telephone, the old series of words used to describe the letters of the alphabet is to be amended by replacing the Jewish names: instead of David, Dora; instead of Jacob, Julius; instead of Nathan, Nikolaus; instead of Samuel, Siegfried; instead of Zacharias, Zeppelin. The Prussian police report that the secret police have received the right to investigate post-office boxes, and letters and packages awaiting delivery in post offices. It has been known for some time that the secret police have been investigating contents of safety deposit vaults, opening the mails, listening to telephone conversations, and are prepared to search the premises of suspicious persons. An American banking representative was arrested last week, but released after a few hours' investigation. Other American banking representatives here are prepared for search and the investigation of all details of their business. Police have made numerous arrests of retailers who have raised prices in an unjustified manner, particularly of butter and other fats. Two hundred arrests were made in Munich at the end of May for this. The Association of Exhibitors at Fairs and Markets has discussed the question of allowing Jews to exhibit their wares in such public places. No general rule has been adopted, but the local authorities in a number of districts prohibit Jews from occupying stands in public markets or exhibiting in fairs; for example, the Frankfort Easter Fair, and the public markets in Darmstadt.

The Organization of Retail Stores continues with its protests against department stores. The final position of department stores is not to be settled until October first. After July first, department stores are to cease competing with artisans, particularly in repair work. This means that they will not be allowed to repair jewelry, clothing, shoes, furniture, or to engage in trades, such as photography. They are also forced to reduce their refreshment rooms and are not allowed to serve special menus or to operate such rooms in any way which differs from the practices of ordinary restaurants. The retail dealers are now demanding that such refreshment rooms be entirely closed, that all grocery departments be closed, and that the department stores be further forbidden to sell books and stationery, tobacco products, and similar articles which are in competition with special retail stores. It is planned in general to restrict department stores to the sale of textile products, clothing, and possibly furniture, as reported earlier.

Preparations for the compulsory work year are going forward. It is planned that by December first, one thousand six hundred and twenty labor groups will be organized with three leaders apiece, naturally chosen from the party. These leaders are now being disciplined and instructed in their duties, so that beginning on January first they will be able further to instruct the new groups of nineteen-year-old boys, who will be brought into the compulsory labor battalions on that date. There is reported to be a tremendous demand for places as leaders of these groups, while there is a noticeable slackening of persons willing to join the labor battalions as ordinary workers.

In the recent annual meeting of the Feldmuehle Paper Company, there was a complaint that the sale of newsprint had been very much reduced through the prohibition of many daily and other newspapers. The process of organizing racial bureaus to pass upon the racial antecedents of individuals is going on. The government office for racial questions, staffed by experts, has been established with branches all over the country. A number of professors of this subject have been appointed in various universities, and a new science is developing. This matter is of great importance in business, since firms which are not able to meet the requirements as German and Aryan firms are shut out of bidding on any kind of public business, and cannot supply any articles which are used by the government, cities and other public bodies. Furthermore, it is planned to introduce a special German trademark to distinguish pure German goods. This will naturally be of great advantage in domestic sales, and it is to apply to all classes of merchandise.

A great deal of discussion has arisen as to how far firms set up with foreign capital can be considered as German. The party leaders have shown themselves rather liberal on this point and insist that goods manufactured in Germany are not to be denied the right to be called German goods merely because the company operates with foreign capital. This does not, however, prevent purely German competitors from making full use of this information in their statements to the public, and there will remain considerable handicaps for the foreign-owned firm. More serious, however, is the situation of a firm which is not considered Aryan, namely, one with Jewish participants. The rules set up to determine what is a non-Aryan firm are as follows:

Partnerships. In a partnership, the greater part of the business management and of the power of attorney must be in the hands of Aryans if the exclusion of non-Aryan influence is to be assured. Non-Aryan partners may be allowed only if they are excluded from the business management and power of attorney.

Limited Partnerships. For limited partnerships the same rules apply as for open partnerships.

Limited Liability Companies. The assurance of the exclusion of non-Aryan influence in a limited liability company exists normally only if the business management is in the hands of Aryans. In addition it appears necessary that the business shares, both by capital and by votes, be mostly in the hands of Aryans. If a limited liability company has a supervisory board, the same rules apply to it as to the supervisory board of a stock company. If special reasons of national economy prevail, a limited liability company can have in addition to two or more Aryan business managers, one or more non-Aryan managers, who in general, however, are entitled to power of attorney only in conjunction with one of the Aryan managers. The majority of managers must always be Aryans.

Stock Companies. The exclusion of non-Aryan influence in a stock company normally seems to be assured only if the president of the supervisory board and the majority of its members are Aryans. Out of the board of directors more than half of the members must be Aryan. In spite of the fulfillment of these premises a stock company must be considered as under non-Aryan influence when more than half of the capital stock is proven to be in non-

Aryan hands. Companies whose stock is made out to the name of the holder must keep files to show the distribution of the stock.

Joint Stock Companies. Joint stock companies are subject to the same rules as stock companies. An undertaking in which the exclusion of non-Aryan influence appears assured through the fulfillment of the above rules is yet to be treated as non-Aryan if it turns out that the undertaking is under the definite influence of one or more non-Aryans.

In addition to the various voluntary funds which have been set up to receive contributions such as the amnesty payments of persons suspected of tax evasion and the special fund for victims of industrial accidents, a new *Hitler-Spende* has been established by the German Manufacturers' Association and the employers' associations. All firms represented in these groups have been told this week to contribute the sum of one-half of one per cent of their total wage bill in the year 1932. The notice is sent by the associations themselves, and interestingly enough it does not give any particulars as to the purpose for which the money will be used. The firms have simply to pay and ask no questions; neither is there any indication of what may happen to a recalcitrant firm which fails to make its expected contribution. This is entirely unnecessary, as everybody knows what is healthy. The amount is not excessive in any individual case, but both German and foreign firms fear, and probably rightly, that this is only the beginning and that they will have to pay and keep on paying for the right to remain in business for some time to come. Incidentally these measures affect foreign-owned as well as German firms with equal severity.

The outward appearance of Germany has been somewhat altered by recent political developments. Both country and city districts have a holiday air. There are many flags, banners, and brown uniforms to be seen, with any number of large and small parades, particularly on week ends. Jews and foreigners are noticeably less numerous and conspicuous in public places. There are more country people to be seen. It is quite obvious that the middle-class people and the country people are having their day. In some public places appear signs: "German Women Do Not Smoke." Last week over the radio, a speaker exhorted German women to abandon the use of cosmetics. There has been a noticeable increase in the number of homespun garments, particularly in the blue color favored by Queen Luise, and the department stores have laid in large stocks. Apparently the belief obtains that there is a certain amount of merit gained by the adoption of old-fashioned styles.

9

CONSOLIDATION OF NAZI POSITIONS

Berlin, August 1, 1933

IN THE LAST TWO MONTHS the leaders of the National Socialist party have been busy strengthening their organization and digging in to protect what they have gained in the first six months of their taking office. Hitler and his immediate lieutenants have been desperately engaged in trying to check further revolutionary activities. Once the masses are aroused and moving, it is hard to stop them, and Hitler is too shrewd to let his followers get out of hand this early in the game. All attempts at a second revolution are frowned on by the authorities, and they are so far successful in quieting the murmurs of their followers.

The success of this retarding policy cannot be measured until next winter. Then, if the business situation has not greatly improved, it may be expected that new revolutionary trends will develop in the S.A. and S.S. and other elements of the party. Such insurgence would take the form of complaints that the leaders of the movement had "got theirs." In other words, Hitler, Goering, Goebbels and company have all reached their personal objectives, while the average S.A. man has still to see what he gets out of it personally. Only in the light of future developments will it be seen whether the revolution has been permanently checked.

In the meantime the government is not inactive. Hitler is very busy putting out new decrees, organizing the four *Staende*, or estates, and getting rid of the last vestiges of Jewish influence and control. As Feder, the Assistant Secretary of Commerce, explained this week privately, the party has four objectives and has promised its followers action in all these four points:

1. Breaking the Versailles Treaty;
2. Restoring Germany's military superiority;
3. Ridding the country of the "Jewish pest";
4. Ending the "International Jewish" capitalistic system.

It is obvious, continued Feder, that the first two objectives cannot be reached right away, as this requires the acquiescence of other countries, and the party must wait until Germany becomes stronger. As for the last two objectives, the party may still go ahead at full speed.

Hitler has made no attempt to conceal his desire to wipe out the Jews from every position of importance. In particular, the big Jewish bankers are going to be thrown out. The Mosse publishing house has gone into bankruptcy and Ullstein will probably follow before long. Georg Tietz and the rest of his family will be forced out of their department stores, and all Jews might just as well make up their minds to kiss good-bye any position of prominence which they may still hold. If they continue to live in Germany at all, they will do so only in the most modest of circumstances. The government states privately that it has been extremely mild in its treatment of the Jews for the last two months, on the whole, in the expectation that foreign propaganda and boycotts against Germany might slacken off. But this has not occurred; and the government has now decided to go ahead with its original plan, since there is nothing to be gained by a policy of mildness.

The most serious charge against the new government, however, is that it has deliberately and officially abandoned certain standards of conduct which have been cherished by all so-called civilized nations for centuries. The government has deliberately introduced practices which have not been openly carried on by any civilized government since medieval times. To these belong the punishment of the innocent as hostages for the guilty. For example, when ex-Minister Philipp Scheidemann published an article in the *New York Times* against the government here, it was officially announced that five of his relatives had been put in concentration camps and would be punished, since he himself was outside Germany. A smaller incident of the same kind occurred this week when, after somebody had, during the night, sawed down a small oak tree planted with much ceremony last Mayday and dedicated to Hindenburg, the German government announced that all communist prisoners in the concentration camps—and there must be many thousands of them—would be deprived of their mid-day meals. Today occurred the first actual executions based only upon political and not civil crimes. Four communists were executed in Hamburg; their crime was simply that they were communists and had taken part in communistic activity. There was no charge against them that they had actually killed anybody. Up to now public executions have been confined only to persons who were definitely accused of deeds of violence.

The government has also publicly announced that wealthy persons placed in concentration camps will be expected to pay for their keep—and not only for themselves, but for enough of their fellow-inmates so that the taxpayers will not be called upon to pay the cost of confining these political prisoners. If this is the definite principle on which the government is acting, one does not need a gift of prophecy to see that there will always be enough wealthy persons incarcerated to keep the camps paying their way. The government has also adopted the principle of cruel and unusual punishments. These barbarous practices, publicly announced by the German government, have not been denied, and there is no need to repeat the excited tales of witnesses to individual violence which may, or may not, be true. The official statements of the government are alone enough to condemn it.

The government is placing great emphasis upon the reduction of unemployment and is having a certain amount of success. This has been partly achieved by seasonal tendencies, partly by the giving of contracts for public construction, partly by removing Jews, socialists and communists and so forth from their positions and filling them with others, partly by provisions forbidding employers to put part-time workers on full time, partly by greater severity in listing persons as unemployed and paying them doles. All in all, a certain small improvement in the business situation is taking place, mostly based upon government construction, but entirely inadequate to help Germany out of her slump and to reduce unemployment by any substantial amount next winter. In allotting new positions, preference is given to National Socialist party members, in order of their joining the ranks; those having party cards with a number below 100,000 are especially preferred.

Certain regulations of the government are directed against the use of machinery in trades where handwork may replace them; for example, the Thuringian glass industry is not allowed to replace glass blowers with any more machines, and hand-made products are to be preferred by buyers. In some cases cigar-making machinery is to be scrapped in factories, according to a recent decree, and in others to be employed only on a quota basis. Very sharp regulations have been issued against German firms removing their plants to other countries. There are special taxes, placed last year, on the export of specific machinery, and firms have been forbidden to advertise inside Germany offering employment abroad for special types of workers. Any German factory owner who establishes a factory abroad is to be considered a traitor in his country.

German retail firms are allowed to have a shield displayed in front of their premises, if they are truly German and not Jewish. The shield is to be under glass and has as a sign the *Hakenkreuz* and a sitting eagle, with the words *Deutsches Geschaeft*. These shields are rented from the local S.A. organization, with a yearly charge. Each S.A. formation has the right to collect the rents in a particular district, and there have recently been some heavy fights between rival groups trying to muscle in on their rivals' territory. This illustrates the extent to which the National Socialist movement is a "racket." Certainly it takes that form for many of the leaders. For the great mass of the public it is a crusade in which they are sincerely and honestly participating; but then, every crusade affords the makings of a racket for somebody.

IO

CAMPAIGN AGAINST UNEMPLOYMENT
AND FOREIGN GOODS

Berlin, September 26, 1933

THERE SEEMS TO BE a widespread belief in foreign countries
that although the National Socialist movement has won a complete success in Germany in the political field, it has still to
solve the economic and financial problems which beset Germany, and that the success of the Hitler government will depend upon the way in which it meets, or fails to meet, economic
realities. This point of view stresses the fact that the business
situation in Germany still remains unpromising, and that the
country is still in the grip of world depression. Many persons
go still further, as for example the French Commercial Attaché, who stated last week, in private conversation, that Germany was facing a financial breakdown and that a question
mark must be placed behind the whole National Socialist
movement in view of this impending financial disaster.

I cannot share this point of view. Certainly, we must admit
that the business situation in Germany has not improved sub-

stantially, nor is it likely to improve in the near future. But I do not believe that the National Socialist movement will stand or fall by its economic success in the next few years. Economic laws are for the most part merely expressions of the way people naturally act under given circumstances, if they are free to act according to their best judgment. In National Socialist Germany, businessmen and the public are not free to act as they would act in Western communities; and accordingly, we can say that for the present at least in Germany many economic laws have been repealed.

Persons who predict a speedy breakdown in Germany would be well advised to turn back to old newspaper files and see what predictions of collapse were made for Fascist Italy in the early days of that movement. Economic disasters which would stir the United States to its depths will hardly affect an autocratic government. An increase of a penny in the pound on the income tax in Great Britain causes a whole political party to be thrown out of power and replaced by its opponents, but in a totalitarian state millions of people may starve to death through bad management by government authorities and the government is more strongly entrenched than ever.

The National Socialist movement is primarily based upon moral and emotional factors and only incidentally reinforced by economic motives. As long as the leaders of the movement can point out to their followers that disarmed Germany is in danger from her armed neighbors, and that under present conditions in the world Germans do not have equal chances for satisfying their personal ambitions as compared with persons of foreign countries, this moral stimulus will remain. Economic setbacks can be easily explained as a result of foreign pressure and are not likely seriously to affect the stability of the government.

In fact, the National Socialist leaders have already anticipated the possibility of conditions getting worse, and have told their followers to prepare themselves for a period of privation and sacrifice. People are being taught to take in their belts and like it. The Propaganda Minister, Dr. Goebbels, has just made a public address in which he prophesies that the two million decrease in unemployment this spring and summer will be maintained over the winter; that next summer, in 1934, another two million will be taken off the total and that in the spring and summer of 1935 the last two million unemployed will be drawn into permanent employment and the problem of unemployment will be finally and definitely solved. I believe that the National Socialist leaders are entirely sincere in making this statement; and the chances are that they can make good on their promise, no matter whether the world business situation improves or not.

The principal method by which unemployment will be solved is by spreading work. This will not only reduce the average number of hours per worker; it also means a lowering of the mechanical efficiency of German industry to such an extent that a greater number of persons will be necessary to perform the work which is being done now. The victories over unemployment in East Prussia, Pomerania and Grenzmark Posen-Westpreussen are not due alone to the demand for agricultural labor, but to the shifting of orders for industrial products to local plants operating with a great deal of hand labor. This movement is spreading in Germany and will have the effect of spreading manufacturing into small units all over the country at the expense of large concentrated undertakings. This is all in line with the policy of the National Socialists of increasing the population on the land and in small villages and breaking up the huge cities and industrial centers, which have been the hotbeds of communism and international socialism. Little by little certain types of machine work are being replaced by hand labor. For example, the manufacture of cigars by machinery has been prohibited. Machine-blown bottles and glass are being replaced by hand-blown products. Certain textile machines, for example, machines for sewing on buttons, have been put out of action and the work is now being done by hand labor; similarly hand-looms have been introduced instead of machine looms in the Cologne district. In giving contracts for road-building and repairs, stipulations are made that hand labor is to be used instead of machinery in many cases.

It seems evident that the government will not attempt to go from a machine to a hand-labor basis immediately to the extent necessary to absorb the existing four million unemployed; they are rather proceeding with caution and testing industries in which this action can be taken. But there seems no doubt at all that it is entirely within the power of the government to carry this to a conclusion and to absorb every unemployed person into industry within two years, as it promises. This, of course, means a lowering of the general efficiency and a reduction in the standard of living of the more fortunate classes. Other plans which are helping to solve the unemployment question are the replacement of women by men in industry and the displacement of Jews and part-Jews, who are not considered as members of the nation, but merely as foreigners for whom there is no obligation to provide employment.

All official statements regarding this campaign speak of the struggle against unemployment and never mention the word "autarchy" which was so popular a few months ago. It seems evident that the principle of autarchy has been adopted, but that the use of the word in public is discouraged in order to minimize foreign reprisals. The principles of autarchy are being put into practice now.

There is no need to search back files for citations. I will briefly mention some of the happenings of the past week to illustrate what is going on. The Department of Agriculture has set fixed prices for wheat and rye and at the same time prohibited farmers from sowing a larger acreage of these grains in the future, in order to leave plenty of land free for raising crops that are rich in fats, and fiber-plants for textiles. German scientists have just met to discuss the substitution of home-produced aluminum for imported copper wherever possible. Feder has just announced that the government will stimulate the production of domestic crude petroleum and artificial petroleum, raising the production of the Leuna works from one hundred thousand to two hundred thousand tons per annum. Wool manufacturers have been instructed to put thirty per cent of artificial wool and shoddy in their cloth to minimize the consumption of foreign wool. Plans have been adopted for recovering sulphur from gas in the Ruhr district as a substitute for imported sulphur. A new method has been worked out for extracting more lard from hogs in order to save imports of foreign fats. A lower tariff contingent has been granted to Yugoslavia for prunes, and low-grade pulp prunes from Yugoslavia are brought in for jam for the most part duty-free, thus replacing American prunes which are brought in at a higher rate. In the case of office equipment, duties have been raised to between one thousand and two thousand marks for one hundred kilograms, which is enough to kill foreign business entirely. Duties on lamp bulbs brought in from Japan have been raised from eighty marks to six hundred and one thousand six hundred marks.

This illustrates the trend here, to free Germany from dependence on imported goods, except those products which come from near-by countries in Central Europe. In other words, the country is going voluntarily on a blockade basis, so that in time of war there will be a minimum disturbance to economic activity. This is described as *Raumwirtschaft* or regional economy. The theory is that Germany ought to be the natural center of a territory in Central and Eastern Europe, which is capable of supplying itself with practically all products.

At the same time, the government does not fail to declare its support of export activity, but it is obvious that the chief emphasis is to be laid upon the restriction of imports—and only upon that basis to stimulate exports as much as is possible under these circumstances. It is thus clear that the chief German objection to American products is not against the products themselves. There is no desire to discriminate against the United States. Simply, these products come all the way across the ocean and do not furnish a reliable means of continuous supply in time of war. There seems to be no argument we can make which will offset this fundamental objection, and the obvious conclusion is that we must be prepared to accept a considerable reduction, even in our present low exports to Germany. Another obvious deduction is that we should give no special consideration to German goods in the United States, since there is no corresponding concession to be obtained here.

To summarize briefly: The National Socialist program involves a rearrangement of German agriculture and industry sufficient to take care of the existing unemployed, and a campaign to make Germany and the surrounding Central European countries a self-supporting bloc. Other considerations are to be subordinated to this general plan, including German export interests and the property rights of the possessing classes if necessary. It is not necessary, in order to secure this objective, that the world business depression be overcome, although any improvement in the business situation will be of assistance; the chief problem for the German government is not one of improving economic conditions, but rather of maintaining the enthusiasm and the discipline of its followers. This is the chief reason why we have seen such an unparalleled series of public meetings, parades, special holidays and intensive propaganda. There seems little doubt that the National Socialist government will be successful in maintaining its hold upon a sufficient number of German people to retain power and accomplish its immediate program. Skeptical foreign criticism should be discounted, as it is based upon a failure to apprehend the circumstances which exist in Germany and the strong moral support which the National Socialist government is now receiving from the public. Very possibly, Americans would not react in the same way, but that is quite beside the point and should not affect our judgment of what the future here will bring.

I I

AMERICAN BUSINESS INTERESTS
IN GERMANY

Berlin, November 18, 1933

AMERICAN SHORT-TERM CREDITS, advanced principally by our larger banks, made up the greater portion of the funds included under the two Standstill Agreements of 1932 and 1933. These sums came to a total of over six billion marks at the end of 1931. Repayments have now reduced the total to between two and one-half and three billion marks, of which the American share still remains the largest. Individual American banks have correspondingly reduced their advances here by more than half and in some cases by two-thirds in the last two years. It is significant that of the remaining credits, more than one billion are made up of acceptance credits which are largely self-liquidating and cover for the most part Germany's current takings of foreign materials, for example, cotton. This type of business is necessary, fairly safe and profitable to the lending banks and will, no doubt, be continued. This means that the amount of short-term advances under the Standstill Agreement, for which pressure still exists for return to the home countries, does not amount to much more than one billion marks at the present time; not a large sum for a country the size of Germany. Most of the Standstill credits which have been repaid up to the present time have been handled at par, so that only very small losses have been taken by the American banks, while the outstanding credits were earning at first six per cent and at the present time pay five per cent under the Agreement. It would seem that American bank advances of this character have not proved to be a particularly bad investment. Furthermore, with the repayment of such a large proportion the position of the remainder looks better; and it is quite possible that before these sums are all repatriated, foreign bankers will not desire to call them home and may even be willing to advance fresh sums. Indeed, they may be called upon to do this under the provisions of the Standstill Agreement, which stipulates that the existing lines of credit must be maintained even though they are not being used to the full. The German government and banks have been extremely careful to treat foreign creditors in this field with great consideration, as it is vital to the country that its credit in this particular be maintained in order to insure the continued movement of necessary foreign commodities.

Dollar Bonds

It has been roughly estimated by banks of issue that of the one billion two hundred million dollars of German dollar bonds at one time held in the United States, three hundred million dollars or approximately one-quarter has been repatriated to Germany. This movement is still going on, particularly to fulfill clauses in the loan contracts which stipulate that a certain proportion of the bonds should be periodically retired, partly to allow German landowners to pay off their mortgages at present attractive rates, and partly to allow German exporters to take advantage of the spread between the local and foreign price of such bonds as a method of quoting lower export prices. This repatriation movement has had the effect of holding up the price in New York and has been about the only factor opposed to the heavy liquidation movement among American owners. Present quotations of German bonds in New York would indicate that these investments, while now showing a heavy loss to the investor, do not compare so very unfavorably with other similar long-term investments made several years ago. On the other hand, the German borrower is stimulated to repurchase these bonds not only because of the present low quotations, but on account of the depreciation of the dollar. Germany cannot afford to buy back too many of the bonds now, as funds are limited, but the deal in the long run is extremely profitable, as the price in New York translated into marks runs in most cases less than one-quarter of the original sums borrowed. Under these circumstances it would seem advisable for American holders not to part with their bonds at low prices but to await higher prices if they can hold on for five or ten years.

Miscellaneous American Investments

American owners of balances in German banks credited for sums due on sales of securities or real estate are in an unfavorable position. Their money is blocked in German banks and can be transferred only by taking heavy losses. The discount, of course, varies on different types of transactions. It is running around twenty-three per cent now for registered marks, but has been as high as thirty per cent.* The discount on *Effekten* marks, which arises from the sale of securities or real estate, has been as high as forty-five per cent, but is showing a tendency to decline. American owners of German securities are also in an unfavorable position. Industrial stocks in Berlin have been declining, the monthly stock index is now at 61.57 (week ending November 11) as compared with 64.57 at the beginning of the year (January monthly average). Holders of mortgage bonds are a little better off on current quotations but face possible declines owing to the uncertainty of government policy regarding farm mortgages. The present tendency here is to relieve farmers as far as possible from their mortgage indebtedness. How far the State will assume these obligations is still problematical.

American Exporters

American firms which have sold goods to Germany or are still engaged in this business face serious difficulties in attempting to transfer funds to the United States. The government foreign-exchange regulations limit every German importer to a foreign-exchange quota which cannot exceed twenty-five per cent of the amount imported by the same firm in the year 1930 or previously. In some cases the quotas allotted are much below this figure. This depends on whether government officials consider the imported commodities as dispensable.

* At this time, the following currencies were used in Germany:
  1. *Reichsmarks*, or marks in general circulation.
  2. Registered marks, sold at a discount to foreign tourists.
  3. *Effekten* marks, currency acquired by the sale of securities or real estate, usually blocked for five years from time of acquisition.
  4. Credit- or *Kredit-Rueckzahlungs* marks, currency acquired by the sale of foreign goods, also blocked.
  5. Free marks, ordinary unblocked currency.

American creditors in this field are uncertain as to how long they can continue to build up balances in Germany which are untransferable according to present regulations. Furthermore, the risk of keeping large unpaid consignment stocks or large sums owing on account is great, as this adds to the ordinary exchange risk and to the credit risk on the importing firm. For this reason a number of American exporters are requesting that their German debtors currently transfer sums owed to the account of the American firm in a German bank, thus building up blocked accounts. Some of these accounts are quite large at the present time and the German government is very loath to give permission to transfer the money out of the country, as it feels that this will stimulate the foreign exporters to send in more goods and build up new credit balances here. This reluctance of the government is extremely pronounced in cases where the merchandise is highly competitive.

American Business Establishments in Germany

Many American firms are maintaining manufacturing or sales establishments in Germany itself, generally owned and operated by subsidiary companies. These firms are at present undergoing great difficulties which may be roughly classified:

1. General difficulty of doing business with present low purchasing power and lack of demand. This requires no further explanation.

2. Open or concealed opposition to foreign goods. This takes the form of a host of published and unpublished regulations prohibiting public bodies from purchasing goods in whole or in part of foreign origin or manufactured by a company owned abroad. It also takes the form of a campaign organized by National Socialist groups and particularly trade

association executives who by pressure force dealers and importers to drop foreign lines. This pressure is accompanied by vague threats of taking the matter up with the National Socialist party and while no specific violence is mentioned, cautious businessmen are only too easily influenced in this way, nor can anyone blame them. In some cases these threats are sent to importers, in others to local dealers throughout the country; and in cases where the foreign firm deals directly with the ultimate consumer, the customer himself is threatened. Furthermore, people nowadays are afraid of purchasing conspicuous foreign goods, as this will give the impression that they are only lukewarm in national sympathy. Specific threats are not needed. It is extremely difficult to combat this type of activity. It originates partly from political sources and to a great extent is stimulated by German companies who are competitors and who seize the chance to use party feeling to help their own business. Such firms are also heavily contributing to the National Socialist campaign funds.

3. Another difficulty for foreign firms as well as German firms now lies in the labor field. The most important effect upon the average firm operating in Germany under the National Socialist government has up to now been the change in relations between the firm and its own employees. Every firm of any size at all must contain a Nazi Cell or unit of the National Socialist *Betriebszellen-Organisation*. This cell is often large enough to include all employees, but sometimes embraces only a few key persons. Where no persons in the organization are considered suitable to head such a cell, the employer has been forced to go outside the organization and hire one or two good party men. Such cells, managed by an *Obmann* or head man, are encouraged to report to the party everything which their conscience may suggest and to exert a strong moral influence, in particular regarding the employ-

ment or retention of National Socialist sympathizers. It is practically impossible for a German employer nowadays to fire a Nazi, and almost every person fired turns out to be a Nazi, even if he were not one the day before. This state of affairs certainly does not encourage efficiency and is steadily weakening the hold of the companies upon their own staffs. The cells are taking increasing part in directing the affairs of their respective companies; they go over the books, pass upon all types of expenditures and advise on general policy. In some cases this is working out very well, in others disastrously. The unfortunate American company which is losing money every day but cannot fire any of its staff must go on losing money as long as it has any assets in the country. There are quite a number of American firms here that at the present time are simply living on their stocks of merchandise and bank balances, and when these are exhausted the firm will go into bankruptcy and the American managers take a quick trip across the frontier, possibly in advance of the final collapse. Several such quick departures have already taken place. American firms losing money here have sometimes considered the possibility of voluntary bankruptcy, but this offers little attraction as it is likely to be strung out over at least two years in the case of an important firm and is certain to result in the loss of practically all the assets. Most firms in this position are simply hanging on now, hoping for a turn in the tide before their reserves are all gone.

4. Foreigners now living in Germany are being subjected to increasing pressure from the tax authorities. Under the old tax laws, dating back to 1923, every person resident in Germany must pay income and capital tax on capital or income outside the country. This law has largely been a dead letter but is being more sharply enforced in recent weeks. Many Americans who were previously let alone have been getting tax notices and

are in some alarm, particularly as they have not been paying taxes on such non-German property or income for many years. American residents and firms here are also subjected to increasing demands for so-called voluntary contributions for National Socialist purposes. The number and variety of these demands appears to be continually increasing. There is no way to compound them in large payments since the fertile brains of the Nazi leaders are thinking up new appeals for cash every day. This is one of the most characteristic features of present-day Germany. Luckily, up to the present time, most of these demands could be met by fairly small gifts. In some cases the amount is determined by a prescribed standard, for example, the *Adolf Hitler-Spende* of the German industry, including foreign companies, was set this year at one-half of one per cent of the total wage bill of the year 1932.

12

HITLER AND THE STABILITY OF
EASTERN EUROPE

Berlin, November 29, 1933

AMERICAN BUSINESS INTERESTS in Germany and surrounding
European countries, as well as the large number of American
investors who have funds tied up in this part of the world, are
interested in the future possibilities and particularly the likelihood or unlikelihood of war or political disturbances in any of
these countries. The present German government is loudly
and emphatically protesting its peaceful intentions, but at the
same time there are many lines of evidence which would seem
to indicate that the National Socialist movement is not inclined to settle down peacefully and turn its attention only to
improving Germany's situation within its own frontiers.

Very often references are made to the statements of Chancellor Adolf Hitler in his celebrated book, *Mein Kampf*. This
book, originally written during his imprisonment in 1924, has
since been revised by him several times. Quotations from the

book in this report follow the German text as published in 1933—the fifty-fourth printing.

The book is the major work of the National Socialist movement and is recommended to all party members. Over seven hundred and fifty thousand copies have been sold in Germany. To date, translations of parts of the book have appeared in both the United States and Great Britain, but these English editions are very much abridged and omit many of the most significant passages. As a matter of record and for the information of the Bureau of Foreign and Domestic Commerce, I am submitting an *exact* and *literal* translation of portions of the book which deal with foreign policy, more particularly with the desire of the National Socialists to readjust their frontiers on the East. It is this oft-repeated desire which has caused so much uneasiness and distrust among Germany's near neighbors.

The careful reading of *Mein Kampf* and similar National Socialist books, newspapers, and pamphlets which have appeared in the past several years, certainly gives an unprejudiced observer the feeling that the German government is probably insincere in its alleged devotion to peace. Indeed, Hitler himself in *Mein Kampf* advocates the use of deception and false statements in propaganda and foreign policy. He believes that the end justifies the means and that such methods should be employed, if necessary, to secure results. After this frank statement of policy, outsiders are certainly not to be blamed if they view the government's protestations of peaceful intention with a certain amount of skepticism.

On the other hand, we should also examine skeptically the inflammatory statements which Hitler makes regarding foreign policy and Germany's mission to expand in the East. Are these statements really complete evidence of National Socialist aggressiveness in foreign affairs or do they merely strike an attitude which is designed to attract patriotic Germans to the movement and give it a popular hold on conservative opinion, which might otherwise be alienated by the radical character of the movement? I think there is some justification for believing that a great deal of the Nazis' war talk, superman talk and posing is simply designed to impress their own followers and should be heavily discounted.

An accumulation of evidence tends to show that the chief policy of the Nazis and their unchangeable principle is to obtain just as much power and authority over the German people as they can and to hold it by all possible means. I doubt very much whether they have many fundamental principles for which they will be prepared to make sacrifices. They are quite ready to adopt any principles which may suit their needs at the moment. They are good opportunists, and are not troubled by charges of inconsistency. There are appended the following quotations from *Mein Kampf*, German edition:

Pages 143-50

"Germany has an annual increase in population of nearly nine hundred thousand souls. The difficulty of feeding this army of new citizens must grow greater from year to year and ultimately end in catastrophe, unless ways and means are found to forestall the danger of starvation and misery in time.

"There are four ways of avoiding so terrible a development for the future:

"1. Following the French example, the increase of births could be artificially restricted, thus meeting the problem of overpopulation. . . .

"For as soon as procreation as such is limited and the number of births diminished, the natural struggle for existence which leaves only the strongest and healthiest alive is obviously replaced by the obvious desire to 'save' even the weakest and most sickly at any price, and this plants the seed of a future generation which must inevitably grow more and more deplorable the longer this mockery of Nature and her will continues.

"And the end will be that such a people will some day be deprived of its existence on this earth; for man can defy the eternal laws of the will to conservation for a certain time, but sooner or later vengeance comes. A stronger race will drive out the weak, for the vital urge in its ultimate form will, time and again, burst all the absurd fetters of the so-called humanity of individuals, in order to replace it by the humanity of Nature which destroys the weak to give his place to the strong.

"2. A second way would be internal colonization. . . . When a people limits itself to internal colonization because other races are clinging fast to greater and greater surfaces of this earth, it will be forced to have recourse to self-limitation at a time when the other peoples are still continuing to increase. Some day this situation will arise, and the smaller the living space at the disposal of the people, the sooner it will happen. Since in general, unfortunately, the best nations, or, even more correctly, the only truly cultured races, the standard-bearers of all human progress, all too frequently resolve in their pacifistic blindness to renounce new acquisitions of soil and content themselves with 'internal' colonization, while the inferior races know how to secure immense living areas in this world for themselves—this would lead to the following final result:

"The culturally superior, but less ruthless races, would in consequence of their limited soil, have to limit their increase at a time when the culturally inferior but more brutal and more natural peoples, in consequence of their greater living areas, would still be in a position to increase without limit. In other words: some day the world will thus come into possession of the culturally inferior but more active men.

"Then, though in a perhaps very distant future, there will be but two possibilities: either the world will be governed according to the ideas of our modern democracy, and then the weight of any decision will result in favor of the numerically stronger races, or the world will be dominated in accordance with the laws of the natural order of force, and then it is the peoples of brutal will who will conquer, and consequently once again not the nation of self-restriction.

"No one can doubt that this world will some day be exposed to the severest struggles for the existence of mankind. In the end, only the urge for self-preservation can conquer. Beneath it so-called humanity, the expression of a mixture of stupidity, cowardice, and know-it-all conceit, will melt like snow in the March sun. Mankind has grown great in eternal struggle, and only in eternal peace does it perish.

"3. Either new soil could be acquired and the superfluous millions sent off each year, thus keeping the nation on a self-sustaining basis; or we could

"4. Produce for foreign needs through industry and commerce, and defray the cost of living from the proceeds. . . .

"The healthier way of the two would, to be sure, have been the first.

"The acquisition of new soil for the settlement of the excess population possesses an infinite number of advantages, particularly if we turn from the present to the future."

Page 738

"The boundaries of the year 1914 mean nothing at all for the German future. Neither did they provide a defense of the past, nor would they contain any strength for the future. Through them the German nation will neither achieve its inner integrity, nor will its sustenance be safeguarded by them, nor do these boundaries, viewed from the military standpoint, seem expedient or even satisfactory, nor finally can they improve the relation in which we at present find ourselves toward the other world powers, or, better expressed, the real world powers."

Pages 739-40

"As opposed to this, we National Socialists must hold unflinchingly to our aim in foreign policy, namely, to secure for the German people the land and soil to which they are entitled on this earth.

And this action is the only one which, before God and our German posterity, would make any sacrifice of blood seem justified: before God, since we have been put on this earth with the mission of eternal struggle for our daily bread, beings who receive nothing as a gift, and who owe their position as lords of the earth only to the genius and the courage with which they can conquer and defend it; and before our German posterity in so far as we have shed no citizen's blood out of which a thousand others are not bequeathed to posterity. The soil on which some day German generations of peasants can beget powerful sons will sanction the investment of the sons of today, and will some day acquit the responsible statesmen of blood-guilt and sacrifice of the people, even if they are persecuted by their contemporaries.

"And I must sharply attack those folkish pen-pushers who claim to regard such an acquisition of soil as a 'breach of sacred human rights' and attack it as such in their scribblings. One never knows who stands behind these fellows. But one thing is certain, that the confusion they can create is desirable and convenient to our national enemies. By such an attitude they help to weaken and destroy from within our people's will for the only correct way of defending their vital needs. For no people on this earth possesses so much as a square yard of territory on the strength of a higher will or superior right. Just as Germany's frontiers are fortuitous frontiers, momentary frontiers in the current political struggle of any period, so are the boundaries of other nations' living space. And just as the shape of our earth's surface can seem immutable as granite only to the thoughtless soft-head, but in reality only represents at each period an apparent pause in a continuous development, created by the mighty forces of Nature in a process of continuous growth, only to be transformed or destroyed tomorrow by greater forces, likewise the boundaries of living spaces in the life of nations.

"State boundaries are made by man and changed by man.

"The fact that a nation has succeeded in acquiring an undue amount of soil constitutes no higher obligation that it should be recognized eternally. At most it proves the strength of the conquerors and the weakness of the nations. And in this case, right lies in this strength alone. . . .

"Much as all of us today recognize the necessity of a reckoning with France, it would remain ineffectual in the long run if it represented the whole of our aim in foreign policy. It can and will achieve meaning only if it offers the rear cover for an enlargement of our people's living space in Europe. For it is not in colonial acquisitions that we must see the solution of this problem, but exclusively in the acquisition of a territory for settlement, which will enhance the area of the mother country, and hence not only keep the new settlers in the most intimate community with the land of their origin, but secure for the total area those advantages which lie in its unified magnitude.

"The folkish movement must not be the champion of other peoples, but the vanguard fighter of its own. Otherwise it is superfluous and above all has no right to sulk about the past. For in that case it is behaving in exactly the same way. The old German policy was wrongly determined by dynastic considerations, and the future policy must not be directed by cosmopolitan folkish drivel. In particular, we are not constables guarding the well-known 'poor little nations,' but soldiers of our own nation.

"But we National Socialists must go further. The right to possess soil can become a duty if without extension of its soil a great nation seems doomed to destruction. And most especially when not some little nigger nation or other is involved, but the Germanic mother of life, which has given the present-day world its cultural picture. Germany will either be a world power or there will be no Germany. And for world power she needs that magnitude which will give her the position she needs in the present period, and life to her citizens."

* * * *

"And so we National Socialists consciously draw a line beneath the foreign policy tendency of our pre-War period. We take up where we broke off six hundred years ago. We stop the endless German movement to the south and west, and turn our gaze toward the land in the east. At long last we break off the colonial and commercial policy of the pre-War period and shift to the soil policy of the future.

"If we speak of soil in Europe today, we can primarily have in mind only Russia and her vassal border states.

"Here Fate itself seems desirous of giving us a sign. By handing Russia to Bolshevism, it robbed the Russian nation of that intelligentsia which previously brought about and guaranteed its existence as a state. For the organization of a Russian state formation was not the result of the political abilities of the Slavs in Russia, but only a wonderful example of the state-forming efficacity of the German element in an inferior race. . . . The giant empire in the east is ripe for collapse. And the end of Jewish rule in Russia will also be the end of Russia as a state. We have been chosen by Fate as witnesses of a catastrophe which will be the mightiest confirmation of the soundness of the folkish theory.

"Our task, the mission of the National Socialist movement, is to bring our own people to such political insight that they will not see their goal for the future in the breath-taking sensation of a new Alexander's conquest, but in the industrious work of the German plow, to which the sword need only give soil."

Page 753

"If the National Socialist movement frees itself from all illusions with regard to this great and all-important task, and accepts reason as its sole guide, the catastrophe of 1918 can some day become an infinite blessing for the future of our nation. Out of this collapse our nation will arrive at a complete reorientation of its activity in foreign relations, and, furthermore, reinforced within by its new philosophy of life, will also achieve outwardly a final stabilization of its foreign policy. Then at last it will acquire what England possesses and even Russia possessed, and what again and again induced France to make the same decisions, essentially correct from the viewpoint of her own interests, to wit: A political testament.

"The political testament of the German nation to govern its outward activity for all time should and must be:

"Never suffer the rise of two continental powers in Europe. Regard any attempt to organize a second military power on the German frontiers, even if only in the form of creating a state capable of military strength, as an attack on Germany, and in it see not only the right, but also the duty, to employ all means up to armed force to prevent the rise of such a state, or, if one has already arisen, to smash it again.—See to it that the strength of our nation is founded, not on colonies, but on the soil of our European homeland. Never regard the Reich as secure unless for centuries to come it can give every scion of our people his own parcel of soil. Never forget that the most sacred right on this earth is a man's right to have earth to till with his own hands, and the most sacred sacrifice the blood that a man sheds for this earth."

13

RACIAL "THEORIES" AND LEGISLATION

Berlin, December 8, 1933

IN THE LAST FEW YEARS a psuedo-science generally described as racial theory has arisen in Germany. A flood of books, pamphlets and newspaper articles have appeared representing a large amount of research and discussion along these lines. I have for some time been reading and studying this subject because it represents one of the main dogmas of the National Socialist party and has already found practical application in whole series of new laws which can be understood only if we have some idea of the beliefs back of them. Furthermore, these dogmas regarding race are still a fundamental tenet of the Nazi creed and will be reflected from time to time in new legislation which is bound to have an important bearing on the commercial, financial, industrial, agricultural, military, educational, religious and cultural life of the country.

Exponents of this racial theory have drawn to some extent

on British and American writers. Their favorite foreign prophet is Houston Stewart Chamberlain, but they are also fond of quoting from Madison Grant and Lothrop Stoddard. The main elements of the Nazi racial theory are somewhat as follows:

Thousands of years ago mankind was divided into a number of distinct races. These races formed selected types which differed widely from each other in physical and mental characteristics. They may, in fact, have arisen from entirely separate origins. Some races are, however, related to other races. Many of these races possessed valuable and useful traits, but the Nordic race originally inhabiting Scandinavia and northern Germany carried in their blood the only substantial basis of civilization, culture, statesmanship and progress. This Nordic race, of all races of the earth, has alone shown the ability to lead and direct mankind upward and onward. Practically all civilization and culture worthy of the name, no matter where it has arisen, was due to some infusion of Nordic blood and the presence of some group of Nordic aristocrats who provided the upper strata of the peoples in question.

It is claimed that such Nordic infusions explain the rise of ancient Egypt, the origin of Chinese civilization, the rise of Greece and Rome, as well as, of course, the subsequent emergence and development of all the northern European countries and the United States.

Threatened Weakening of Nordic Strain

It is believed by this school of thought that the rise and fall of nations in the past was determined by an infusion and subsequent loss of Nordic blood; that the whole history of the human race since recorded times has been a series of Nordic conquests which have fertilized and fructified various peoples and enabled them to make a contribution to history and that later on this Nordic blood died out through war, restriction of birth, enervating luxuries and principally through mixing with inferior bloods, and that one country and civilization after another decayed when the Nordic strain vanished. It is pointed out that this explains the static civilization of China, the fall of Egypt, Greece and Rome from their former greatness, and that the process of decay is still going on in Italy, France and Spain where it has reached various stages; that there is great danger the Nordic race will finally become an inconsequential minority even in its home countries, notably Germany, Scandinavia, Great Britain, and the United States; and that the final result will be the ultimate extinction of civilization and culture on this planet, since only inferior races will be left alive.

In order to prevent this disaster, these racial theorists believe that a determined effort must be made to increase the number of Nordic children, restrict the birth of inferior racial elements, segregate the Nordic elements in each country so that they may breed a pure strain and thus insure permanent improvement and progress. This school of thought also believes that a mixing of races is bad for all concerned, that even the inferior races may have certain good qualities in their pure and unmixed state, but that a mixed population represents a hodge-podge of stunted and lopsided persons whose bodies, minds and souls are out of balance.

For example, Hans Guenther, the high priest of Nazi racial theory, who was appointed by Frick as Professor at the University of Jena in 1930 over the protests of the University authorities, declares in his work *Rassenkunde des deutschen Volkes*, pages 259 to 264, that nearly all persons in modern Europe represent varying racial mixtures. This explains a certain disharmony in their personalities. For example, a man may have inherited large bones and muscles from one race and a small inadequate heart from another. He may have kidneys from one race which are quite unsuitable for his liver. This causes weakness, disease, tendency to appendicitis, tuberculosis and many other physical ailments. Such race mixtures produce homely and unattractive persons with double or multiple personalities. A man may have his imagination from one race and his memory from another. This explains a great many of the bodily and mental ills which afflict mankind. The remedy is to breed pure races again out of the present mixture; and particularly to breed and strengthen the Nordic race, which is the one of importance and value.

Racial Composition of Germany

According to Guenther, the various races represented in present-day Germany are as follows, in round numbers:

Nordic race	50%
Eastern race	20%

By "Eastern" he means light, round-headed, low-statured persons generally classified by anthropologists as the Alpine race.

Dinaric race	15%

By these are meant the Southern Bavarians, tall, dark, with strong features and distantly related to the Semitic peoples.

East Baltic race	8%

By these are meant the Northern Slavs.

"Faelic" race ....about	1%

This is supposed to be a German variety of the main Nordic race, situated principally in Westphalia, and characterized by square-shaped heads and large stature; for example, Hindenburg and Bismarck.

"Western" race 2%

This is identical with the anthropological term, Mediterranean race.

Sudetic race, South Slavs 2%
Inner Asiatic race 2%

The latter means the Jews.

It is interesting to note that the chief authorities for this new racial science do not regard the Jewish race as a particular menace. It is so small in number in Germany as to be of minor importance and to be easily dealt with. It is only in the popular conception of the race theory, which has been widely diffused among the rank and file of the Nazis, that the racial problem becomes one of Aryan against Jew. The real problem which racial theorists propose to tackle is a reduction and eventual elimination of the Eastern or Slavic races from German blood. This is obviously a question of tremendous magnitude, as most impartial foreign authorities assign roughly two-thirds of present-day Germans to the Alpine or Slavic races. It is clear that no popular campaign could ever be inaugurated in Germany eventually to weed out of the national blood strain so large a body of persons. This objective, however, is to be kept in mind and attained through various indirect means, some of which will be described. Most of the legislation on racial matters which the National Socialist government has already adopted is designed merely to promote early marriage and increase the birth rate of all Germans. But this ultimate objective of breeding a Nordic Germany remains at the back of their minds.

Regulations Against Jews

Naturally, the first working-out of racial theory in legislation which occurs to foreign observers is the series of actions against Jews. These are too familiar to require comment. Their general purpose is to remove Jews from commanding positions in trade, the professions and other walks of life, force them into subordinate positions and restrict future growth and importance of the race in Germany. It has been estimated that the larger part of Germany's Jews have already left the country. Those that remain will be relegated to unimportant positions in the community and, it is hoped, will have fewer children.

Loans to Newly Married Couples

As a method of raising the birth rate, the government has granted one thousand marks as a loan to each newly married couple when the wife has given up a position in order to marry. This not only increases the birth rate and puts women back in the homes, but it provides work for more men and relieves unemployment. Over one hundred million marks have already been "loaned." Most of this will never be repaid; in fact, does not have to be repaid if the marriage results in the proper number of children.

Hereditary Peasantry

A law has recently been passed forbidding farmers to sell or mortgage their land or crops and preventing foreclosures on existing mortgages. This affects three-quarters of all the agri-

93

cultural land in Germany. Land is to descend from father to the eldest son and a hereditary peasantry of predominant Nordic blood is to be established on the land. The effects of this law upon agricultural credit and mortgage banks have been so disastrous that the central government is being forced to step in and provide some sort of guaranty for existing mortgages. I have been confidentially informed by the German Ministry of Agriculture that within a few weeks a law establishing a new Guaranty Bank would come out, regulating this situation.

Sterilization of the Unfit

Laws providing for the voluntary or compulsory sterilization of the unfit have been passed. It is estimated that one hundred and thirty thousand persons are immediately available for operations of this kind. Certain extremists would like to use this weapon as a method of getting rid of whole classes of the population; Jews are generally mentioned in this connection, but it is unlikely that any such method will be adopted. How radical the ideas are, will be shown by a reference to *Rassenpflege im voelkischen Staat* by Staemmler, one of the authorities on this subject, quotations from whose book are currently read in the official radio programs as a part of Nazi policy. On page 98 he advocates that children who fail to pass twice in school should be examined and if considered inferior should be sterilized before reaching maturity.

Taxation of Bachelors and the Childless

The existing surtaxes for single persons, both men and women, are to be retained or increased. In addition, the whole taxation program is to be remodeled so as to press with particular severity upon those persons who are not producing their proper quota of children. Staemmler advocates on pages 74 to 86 of his book *Rassenpflege im voelkischen Staat* that a quota of children be assessed for each class of the population, based among other things on income. Thus a married man with an income of two hundred and fifty dollars a month would be assessed at a normal quota of five children. Any number less than this would call for heavy financial penalties, for example, a married man with such an income and no children would be taxed sixty per cent of his income and the money turned over to families with more children than their quota. The Minister of the Interior, Frick, has already announced that tax plans looking in this general direction are under way.

Other methods by which Staemmler suggests that the number of desirable children would be increased (page 83 of his book) are the arrangement of pensions and promotions for employees according to the number of children. And on page 119 he suggests that only children from large families be allowed to enter the advanced schools and universities and so become qualified for professions and careers. This would effectively counter the racially subversive tendency of parents to restrict families in order that their smaller number of children may get on in the world, and would encourage ambitious parents to qualify their offspring for favorable careers by having a sufficiently large family.

Need for Illegitimate Children

Alfred Rosenberg, head of the Foreign Political Department of the National Socialist party, in his recent book *Der Mythos des 20. Jahrhunderts,* declares that the State needs every possible child of superior race which can be produced. On page

592 he discusses the need for a larger number of illegitimate children of Nordic race and goes on as follows:

"Professor Wieth Knudsen rightly pointed out that without periods of polygamy the German racial strain could never have been established in former centuries, which is to say that the entire basis for the culture of the Western world would otherwise never have existed. This is something which lifts this historical fact out of the realm of moralizing. There have also been other times in which the number of women has greatly exceeded that of man. This is the case today. Shall these millions of women be laughed at and pitied as old maids and go through life robbed of their rights? Shall a hypocritical sex-satisfied society condemn these women to celibacy? A future Germany will deny this. It will, although retaining monogamous marriage, also give the same rights and honors to German mothers of children outside marriage and the social and legal position of illegitimate children will be entirely equal to others.

"The question up to the German people is simply whether it wishes in coming conflicts to conquer or to perish. Therefore, in view of the many childless marriages and the excess of females, if unmarried women produce children it is an increase of strength for the entire German race. We are entering a tremendous struggle for the substance of our race. If this fact is recognized, the consequences must be drawn by the moralists and hypocrites of ladies' societies who knit wrist warmers for niggers and Hottentots and spend money for missions to the Zulus but at the same time protest immorality when a man declares that the preservation of the substance of a race which has been condemned to death is the most important consideration, before which everything else must stand aside, and that this demands the preservation of all healthy German blood. Then a real morality and the preservation of the freedom of the entire nation is unthinkable otherwise. Moral considerations which are good in ordinary periods of peace do not count in times of struggles of destiny. The German empire of the future will, therefore, consider the childless women as an inferior member of society quite equally if she is married or not. But if a German woman mixes with negroes, orientals, Jews, she will have no legal protection either for her legitimate or illegitimate children, for whom the rights of German citizens cannot be claimed. The person of foreign race [committing such an offense], however, should be punished by whipping, imprisonment, loss of property and life-long banishment from the German empire."

Miscellaneous Regulations

Early marriage of Nordics is to be encouraged by reducing the school and university period necessary for preparation for the professions. Agricultural settlements of predominantly Nordic families are to be placed at points on the land where Germanism is in danger, principally on the frontiers. Sale and exhibition of drugs and apparatus for birth control are to be severely restricted. Divorce on grounds of marriage to a non-Aryan becomes legal. A society for those families rich in children (*Bund der Kinderreichen*) has been organized to advocate government subsidies. A government speaker on the German radio recently warned mothers not to allow their little girls to play with black dolls. He said, "Nothing could fill a pure Nordic with such abhorrence as a sight of a little blond girl fondling a pickaninny."

14

NATIONAL SOCIALIST MOVEMENT AT THE END OF 1933

Berlin, December 13, 1933

IN THE CLOSING WEEKS of the year 1933 German affairs have moved into a period of comparative quiet. The campaign against unemployment, which was carried on during the warmer weather, has quieted down, to be resumed again in the spring. Present efforts of the government are more designed to prevent unemployment from increasing over its present figure than to make new jobs at the moment. The more recent campaign of the Winter-help, namely, a collection of voluntary contributions from all parts of the country to relieve need in the winter months, has also become more quiet. The period of large contributions is over and the small regular weekly and monthly collections will now be supplemented only by charity balls, theater performances and the like.

There is one activity, however, which is going steadily forward, i.e., the promotion and extension of the organization of society throughout Germany. This movement is not noisy or exciting, but it is proceeding with thoroughness and spreading all over the country. The evident design of the government is to extend various forms of National Socialist organizations so far as to include practically every person in the country and, if possible, to get hold of each person not only through one but through several channels at the same time.

The Estates

Among these organizations which spread through the country are first the estates, or *Staende*. These, representing the organization of society according to means of livelihood, have been described in previous reports. Probably the most active *Stand* at present is the *Reichsnaehrstand* for agriculture, which has been built up principally by Reichsminister Darré. Parallel to its extension is the growth of the *Reichshandelsstand*, covering trades; this is under the control of von Rentelen. The *Reichsindustriestand* under the leadership of Krupp von Bohlen is also extending its membership. The *Stand* for the free professions has not yet been organized, but the groundwork is being laid and a number of subsidiary organizations have already been formed, which will later be grouped together in this *Stand*. These include the Chamber of Physicians and Surgeons, the Federal Culture Chamber, the Film Chamber, the Press Chamber and so forth. The Ministry of Propaganda is taking a strong interest in this particular field. The interests of workmen are being taken care of in the extension of the German Labor Front, headed by Dr. Ley. This organization plans not only to include the membership of every employed person in the country but through a special department will organize and supervise the spare time of the workers, including the hours after work, vacations and holidays.

Air Raid Defense

Another type of organization which is going forward rapidly is the *Luftschutz* or protection against air raids. It is planned to get hold of one-third of the entire population of the country hereby. Every dwelling-house is eventually to be provided with a bomb-proof and gas-proof cellar. Every house is to have one to three persons with specified duties in time of emergency. Certain persons are to prevent fire, others to marshal the population and to conduct them to the appropriate cellars, and others to give first aid and medical attention. Every block is to be organized into a unit which will stage fire and gas drills. At the present time this movement has just reached the stage where instructors are being taught; every evening hundreds of courses are held in which persons are instructed as teachers for additional classes. After a certain period of time, each person now getting instructions will set up a new class and impart his knowledge to a larger number. In this way, the entire country is to be covered.

Children and Youth

Another method by which all the population is being reached is through the youth, especially those of the poorer classes. Supervised play and children's nurseries, games, sports, singing-societies and so forth, have been called into being. This type of organization runs clear into the smallest villages. They will reach into almost every home and will affect the greater part of the population, both young and old. Indeed, a patriotic and public-spirited Nazi leads an extremely busy life. He is probably a member of a dozen different organizations and his entire time outside working hours is filled with organization duties. Never were so many people running about the streets collecting dues and subscriptions, drumming up members to attend meetings of this and that, distributing handbills and the like. The German people are rather inclined to this sort of activity and do it very well. There is the question, however, whether it is not being overdone at present, and may result in a considerable amount of indifference and in a reaction of public opinion later. However, the public here can probably stand a lot of organization and still like it.

Experiments

The present period is also characterized by a great deal of experimenting, particularly in economic measures. It is quite clear that the National Socialist party has not altogether made up its mind on a number of points, and that divergent interests and personalities inside the party are still struggling with one another. For example, German firms have recently complained that they are uncertain with which government officials to deal. Authoritative letters have been sent out by the *Deutsche Arbeitsfront,* which is headed by Dr. Ley, stating that firms should deal only with him and his organization in all labor matters. At the same time similar letters came from Reichsminister Seldte of the Labor Ministry to the effect that firms must deal only with that organization in labor matters and not with the *Arbeitsfront.* These same firms have also been receiving letters from Keppler, the economic assistant of Hitler, telling them to deal only with him and not with the *Ar-*

beitsfront and the Ministry of Labor. This causes uncertainty and hesitation and may take some time to clear up.

Change of Policy

There also is a certain amount of backing and filling with sharp reversals of policy. For example, the *Deutsche Wochenschau,* a weekly magazine published by Dr. Feder of the *Reichswirtschaftsministerium,* carried at the end of October the statement that members of the National Socialist party were not permitted to purchase in department stores and that any person entering a department store in party uniform would be immediately banned from the party. A few weeks later, the same weekly carried a second article reversing its previous decision and stating that party members could purchase in department stores. Evidently, there had been some very strong representations made to Feder in the meantime.

The truth is that the National Socialist party still remains extremely hostile to department stores, chain stores and the like; but that the government and government-owned banks are for the time being financially interested in the leading department stores, and could not find satisfactory employment for the personnel of such stores if they were shut down, so that this type of store is tolerated, if not liked, until a better opportunity comes for replacing it.

Small-Town Statesmen

The National Socialist movement is also embarrassed by zealous members, particularly in small towns and villages. Some such men have been putting out regulations which are worse than ridiculous. For example, in Lippe a law has been passed forbidding the population to spread margarine on bread, although, apparently, it can be used for other purposes. In Marbeck a milk dealer was placed under arrest because he had decided to give up his business and it was feared that this would endanger the supply of milk to the public. In Saxony the provincial government has thought it necessary to make a declaration against the custom of hanging up public placards which name certain persons as enemies of the nation and warn everyone not to have anything to do with them. Radical ideas in medicine are also being propagated. For instance, at a National Socialist meeting in Berlin, several physicians suggested doing away entirely with the use of animal preparations, with medicines such as glands and gland products; for example, insulin-vaccination, inoculation by serums and the like. It was said that this represents a materialist Marxian view of life and that no animal products should be introduced into human blood. Even the national government from time to time issues orders which seem difficult to carry through. For example, Minister Darré has forbidden any discussion of the law preventing farmers from selling or mortgaging their land.

Gain in Moderate Opinion

At the same time, there are other signs which show that a more reasonable point of view is gaining ground; for example, the declaration of the *Deutsche Arbeitsfront* after the election of November 12, which stated that bygones are bygones and that no workman should be persecuted or looked down upon because of his previous association with the Socialist or Communist party, provided such association had been brought to an end. There still remains, however, a certain antagonism between the old Nazis who had belonged to the movement long before its triumph, and the more recent acquisitions who have joined at the eleventh hour and now have become the majority. This difference in point of view was well illustrated in the last week by a speech from Minister Schmitt of the *Reichswirtschaftsministerium,* who said that in the future it would not matter so much about the membership card, but that the heart of the individual counted. On the very same day, a meeting of National Socialist provincial leaders in Berlin discussed ways and means for retaining control of the movement in the hands of the old Nazis, and giving preference to them in the matter of employment and important duties.

Regional Economy

It is interesting to note that even such a conservative as Dr. Posse, secretary of the *Reichswirtschaftsministerium,* has come out for *Raumwirtschaft* or the building of regional economic blocs. He has recently declared in two public speeches that Germany must abandon the most-favored-nation principle in commercial treaties and develop an economic bloc of which it is the center, surrounded by the smaller countries of Southeastern Europe, and, it is hoped, Holland and Scandinavia. Within this bloc, preferential tariff duties should encourage reciprocal trade.

News Merger Helps Propaganda

An interesting and important development of the last few days is the amalgamation of the two telegraphic news services, *Wolf* and the *Telegraphen-Union,* formerly controlled by

Hugenberg. These two are to be combined in an official telegraphic service with the name "German News Service" (*Deutsches Nachrichtenburo*). This will strengthen the Propaganda Ministry in giving out one official version of everything to the press and will make it more difficult for foreign newspaper correspondents in Berlin, who will either have to accept the official version of every story or attempt to build up their own sources of information. It will, of course, be almost impossible to avoid using the official version, as the government news service will in many instances have a monopoly on the facts.

15

ECONOMIC IDEAS

Berlin, December 18, 1933

WHEN THE NATIONAL SOCIALIST PARTY first obtained power in Germany, one of the first questions raised in the United States was, "What will this mean to business?" A fit answer to this question can best be made by examining what the Nazis have actually done since coming into power, and this has been the subject of a number of reports from this office. But what they are likely to do in the future and what their whole attitude toward business will finally prove to be, cannot be thoroughly understood without some examination of the economic ideas back of the Nazi movement.

It is extremely difficult to form a clear picture of the National Socialist economic theory. The reason is that the party and its leaders are vague and doubtful in their own minds as to what they believe and what they want. This has resulted in all sorts of conflicting statements and mistaken ideas. In fact, the Nazis themselves say that nobody who is imbued with the democratic and liberal traditions of the Anglo-Saxon world can possibly understand their movement. This may be true, for I certainly fail to see clearly any well-defined economic policy in all the welter of National Socialist literature on this subject or in the multitude of speeches which have been broadcast over the country.

Jewish "Plot" to Control the Earth

Perhaps it may be best to say that one cannot understand the National Socialist attitude toward economic questions without believing, as their leaders say they do, in the existence of a world-wide Jewish conspiracy to destroy all that is best in civilization. This Jewish conspiracy is supposed to have its roots back in past centuries and to have gained strength from the rising liberal, democratic, modernistic, materialistic movements of thought in the last one hundred and fifty years. Many other forces unconsciously placed themselves in the service of this conspiracy, for example, the French Revolution, the revolt of the American colonies, the American Declaration of Independence, the rise of industrialism, the growth of scientific doubt in religious and political dogmas, and finally, in more modern days, the rise of Marxist socialism, communism, and as its partner, international finance. To the Nazi mind a Russian communist and a New York or London banker are both members of the same movement, which is striving to sap the foundations of society, weaken the Nordic race, destroy the aristocratic principle, undermine the Christian religion, the obedience of children to their parents, of wives to their husbands, and replace in its stead a mechanized, materialistic, godless world, filled with people of mixed and inferior races, devoted to international trade and the pursuit of wealth and luxury.

Capital Both Good and Evil

Hitler, in his book *Mein Kampf,* traces the outlines of this conspiracy from its early beginning to the final decay of nations and peoples. Gottfried Feder, of the Ministry of Commerce, in his book *Kampf gegen die Hochfinanz* and other books and pamphlets, shows how Jewish capital, acting internationally, has attempted to enslave nations, more particularly Germany, since the war. He draws a distinction between *"schaffendes und raffendes Kapital,"* or between constructive and destructive capital. The latter is principally Jewish capital and capital loaned internationally. It is the capital invested in large enterprises doing international business, incorporated in such form as to escape personal responsibility and working in such large units as to defy control by the law. The international character of such investment capital is a particular menace; it is unpatriotic and seeks to avoid its duties and responsibilities toward the tax authorities and toward the workers; above all, it does not fit into the organic State and does not readily take orders from an inspired national leader, like Hitler.

Large Business Units Not Desired

This last point is the crux of the matter. The Nazi principle of a single authoritative will ruling the State cannot reconcile itself to the existence of large corporations with international interests. The party, since its experience in power, has announced some exceptions to this general rule. Shipping concerns may be large, certain types of manufacturing can be carried on only in large units, but wherever possible such units are to be broken up and made a part of the life of the countryside; in particular all trade is to be handled by small firms. There are to be no such things as large department stores, mail-order houses, large wholesalers, branch stores, co-operative purchasing and selling organizations. This policy is already beginning to make itself felt. The Nazis have prevented the organization of any new enterprises of this kind and in the case of department stores have already taken some lines of business from them, as described earlier.

Loss of Capital by German Companies

The Nazis are encouraging a revival of small manufacturing in country districts, and this is bound to affect large industries seriously. It seems unlikely that the great German firms will be directly attacked by the government, but a mere continuation of existing circumstances is going to sap their resources. On the one hand they are called upon to maintain a padded payroll, whether orders are coming in or not. On the other hand, they are called upon to give heavily to all sorts of so-called voluntary charities as well as pay heavy taxes. At this rate, the liquid capital and reserves of such companies are being eaten up, necessary replacements and alterations cannot be made, and in the course of a few years the great German firms will be nothing but hollow shells with the life-blood sucked out of them, unless a substantial improvement in business, particularly export business, can save them, or unless the government changes its tactics.

Back to Nature

This all points to a reduction in the standard of living of the German people and a decline in Germany's industrial efficiency. Much of what the Nazis have said and done indicates that they are prepared for this and even welcome it. Hitler has rigidly declared for the *Primat der Politik,* or the Primacy of Politics, that is to say, at the present time, political, racial and military questions come first and economic affairs are of secondary importance. It is claimed that too much attention has been paid to raising the standard of living and attempting to seek happiness through material possessions and that the German people will be happier if they lead simpler, healthier, outdoor lives without struggling to obtain the modern so-called conveniences and luxuries. One writer has declared that patched garments will not be considered disgraceful nor a sign of inferiority. More attention is to be paid to folk art and home industries, such as homespun linen, rag rugs, home-made toys, utensils, articles of furniture, etc. This cult has gone so far to alarm businessmen that Hitler, perhaps against his own inclinations, was compelled to call a halt to it some time ago, and in a public speech denied the intention of adopting a *Primitivitaets-Kult*—that is, a principle of primitive living, or *Bolschewistische Beduerfnislosigkeit,* which means the ability to do without things. This utterance of his, however, is not an indication that the general trend in this direction has been or will be stopped. Circumstances may prove too strong, and if the general fabric of production and consumption continues to receive such blows, whether intended or not, the result will be a lower standard of living, quite apart from whether it is accidental or designed.

Future Position of Capitalist Class

There is yet no satisfactory answer to the question of what rôle *schaffendes* or constructive capital will play in a National Socialist Germany. There are to be banks and these will have a certain amount of private initiative. A government commit-tee is now studying the question as to how the banks are to be organized in the National Socialist State, and will report, prob-ably, in a few months. There will be stock exchanges where securities can be bought and sold, although the names of these institutions may be changed just as the *Getreideboerse* has be-come the *Getreide-Grossmarkt*. It is apparently contemplated that a *rentier* class will exist and that there will be an invest-ment capital market. Nazi leaders have for years been agitat-ing against the slavery of interest, but it is not quite clear at what percentage slavery commences, or what is considered a reasonable return on investments. Some authorities claim that two per cent is enough, others set a higher figure, while a few have gone so far as to say that no interest should be paid to private persons at all, though possibly the State should have the right to receive interest on its loans to farmers and other classes of the population.

Leanings Toward Autarchy

Another disputed point of National Socialist theory is the extent to which national self-sufficiency, or autarchy, is to be adopted. Most members of the party are agreed that this is the desirable goal, but there are many differences of opinion as to how far the country can go in this direction without the danger of reprisals from abroad and destruction of values at home. Certainly the great port cities of Hamburg and Bremen, the important import and export districts and the industry which exists on foreign trade will be against autarchy, but the general tendency is still strongly in its direction.

Nazis Imitate Technocracy

Among the more impractical theorists of the movement can be mentioned Dietrich Klagges, author of the book, *Reichtum und soziale Gerechtigkeit,* "Wealth and Social Justice." Klagges has apparently been copying the ideas of technocrats in the United States and has worked out elaborate charts and formulas, reducing all wealth and means of exchange to an energy basis. He and similar theorists have a certain limited following in the party but their ideas do not affect government policy to any apparent extent.

Fixed Prices

Prices of many agricultural products are fixed. Grain prices have been fixed for some time and all wheat and rye are traded in through government channels. This has also been true for a number of other foodstuffs such as maize, rice, fodder, edible fats and oils. According to a cabinet decision of last Friday, government monopolies are to be set up for eggs, butter and cheese, and a schedule of fixed prices is to be published shortly. Rumor has it that milk will be included later. No one can say whether this is a forerunner of fixed prices and monopoly control for all other foodstuffs or not, or whether it is practicable for Germany to put fixed prices on farm products and leave manufactured goods to be regulated by the law of supply and demand.

Less Government Ownership

Both the recent actions of the government and the statements of important Nazis seem to show that the government does not plan to own and operate business enterprises directly.

Two recent instances of this kind have been the turning back to private hands of the government's shares in the Gelsen-kirchen steel industry and the exchange of some of the shares in the Deutsche Bank, which the government possessed, for a large building owned by the Deutsche Bank which has now become government property. Feder in his speech on Saturday stated that the government as the leader of industry could not itself afford to engage in business. This apparently means that National Socialism is not to be confounded with state socialism or public ownership.

Economic Freedom Impossible Under Nazis

The principle of ownership and operation of business by private capital is retained. Nevertheless, this is a distinction without a real difference. A free economic society is impossible without freedom of the individual in political and social matters. Under a government where the individual has no particular rights of his own it becomes a matter of minor importance whether he possesses the title to property in his own name or is merely an employee of the government. This fundamental fact about National Socialism is not well enough understood abroad. We have been so accustomed to discussions regarding our economic rights and the economic structure of society that we are prone to forget that such economic rights are postulated upon the possession of political rights. In National Socialist Germany these political rights of the individual have disappeared. It is no longer of any importance whether the system here is called socialism or private initiative. The government has the right to control the daily life of every person and will direct things in the economic sphere as it sees fit.

What this means can be judged by recent speeches broadcast on the official radio last week. One speaker warned the farmers not to dare to depart from the government instructions regarding the kind of crops they are to sow and the acreage of each. Another one warned German households against the spending of money on personal luxuries at Christmas time. In particular, members of clubs or societies were told not to give Christmas presents to each other but to turn the money over to the National Socialist charities for distribution to the worthy poor. Citizens were particularly urged not to consume beer and pig's knuckles on this Christmas but to give the money usually spent for these delicacies to Nazi collectors. We may be sure that any government which can go so far as to limit such fundamentals of German middle-class existence has both the strength and the inclination to exercise a very direct control over the lives of the individuals.

No Real Parallel With the United States

There has been some tendency in Germany to draw a comparison between the measures of the National Socialist government in 1933 and the acts of the American government during the same period. Superficially there are certain points of resemblance. This is quite natural since both governments were attacking the same fundamental problem, namely, the world-wide business depression, but under the surface there is no similarity. In the United States tremendous efforts are being made to improve economic conditions by economic measures; in Germany the entire political structure and the fundamental law of the land have been completely altered, while the economic changes are on the whole merely incidental. A critical observation of Nazi economic measures fails to find any well-thought-out plan of business reconstruction.

The Nazi campaign against Jews, liberals, foreigners and international capitalists seems very much like a revolt of the stupid and ill-adjusted against a complex modern world in which such persons are finding it increasingly difficult to compete. The Nazi hostility toward the Marxists is easily explained as the bitterness of one set of demagogues trying to discredit their competitors for the allegiance of the masses.

16

NEW GERMAN LABOR CODE

Berlin, January 19, 1934

THE GERMAN PRESS published on January 18 a detailed summary of a new German Labor Code or "Law for the Regulation of National Labor," which was approved by the cabinet in the middle of January, but will not be promulgated in its definite form for some time to come. Nevertheless, the general ideas and provisions of the new law bring such sweeping changes in the whole régime of labor in Germany, and will have such far-reaching influences on industrial conditions in this country, that a brief preliminary survey of its contents appears opportune. The new law will come into effect on May first, 1934, the second German National Labor Day; on this day, employers and employees, who will be appointed to the various new posts provided for by law, will be sworn in with fitting ceremonies all over Germany.

It is impossible to understand the various provisions of the law without taking into account that an attempt is being made by the present German government to put all relations of various social groups within industry and trade on an entirely new basis. Social legislation regulating relations between employers and employees was heretofore based in Germany, as it still is in most other countries of the world, on the assumption that there is an inherent conflict of interests between the two parties or classes concerned—employers and employees. Consequently, the main object of the State, of legislation and administration, was thought to be the leveling out and smoothing of this divergence of interests, and the avoidance, by means of conciliation and arbitration, of such conflicts breaking out into open industrial warfare. The philosophy of National Socialism underlying the new German Labor Code is entirely different. It emphatically refutes the idea of inherent class strife and class warfare, and wants to substitute for it the idea of social solidarity—of co-operation by all engaged in the process of production, regardless of their social position.

This basic conception is supplemented by two other fundamental ideas. In the first instance, the favorite Nazi idea of "leadership" (*Fuehrerprinzip*) has to apply to economic life just as well as to all forms of political and cultural activity. The natural "leader" in industry and trade is the head of an industrial enterprise, the employer, wherefore it is understood that he is tied by links of mutual confidence and loyalty to his "followers"—the employees who are working in his enterprise. The head of a concern or "industrial leader" is, under the new law, granted exceptional powers with the idea of liberating him from the fetters previously imposed upon him by labor unions as well as by employers' associations. In fact, according to the letter of the law, the employer is granted almost dictatorial powers within his own enterprise. These powers are, however, substantially restricted by serious obligations expressed in a principle which is also entirely novel, that of "Social Honor." This "social honor" imposes serious obligations upon all participants in the process of production—toward each other and toward the State. Special "courts of honor" with extremely wide powers are to safeguard the realization of this principle of social honor in daily life. The extent, therefore, to which the seeming autocratic powers of the employer under the new code will be actually restricted largely depends upon the way these courts of honor will exercise their functions.

In the second instance, Nazi economic philosophy considers the factory or the workshop as the real germ-cell of the industrial community. The main attention of the legislator and the administrator has, therefore, to be directed toward creating truly harmonious relations within this cell.

It is one of the interesting features of the new code that most of its provisions are extremely vague, and thus leaves a considerable leeway for the execution of its provisions. It is, therefore, extremely difficult to form an advance opinion as to the actual bearing of the new law, or laws, on industrial conditions in Germany. This will, to a large extent, depend on the spirit in which the law is administered, and on whether the "conservative" or "radical" ideas and elements of the law will prevail in the long run.

The Employer and the Work Council

As already indicated, according to the basic idea of the law, the employer or head of an enterprise is its "undisputed leader." The employees and workmen are his "followers," bound to him by ties of mutual confidence and loyalty. The "leader" alone decides all questions pertaining to the running of the business. He has to look after the welfare of his followers. In factories and works owned by a corporation the latter has to appoint one of its executives as a responsible "leader." This provision will naturally also apply to manufacturing and other subsidiaries owned by foreign concerns. In all enterprises with more than twenty employees, a Work Council or *Vertrauens- rat* has to be formed, which exercises advisory functions only, and of which the "leader" or employer is the chairman. The Work Council has to further the spirit of mutual confidence within the enterprise, to advise the head of the concern in questions relative to the improvement of efficiency, physical protection of the workmen and, in particular, to discuss the general work regulations to be issued by the employer. All persons at least twenty-five years of age, who have belonged to the enterprise for one year and who have been working for at least two years in their respective branch of industry, can be nominated members of the Council (*Vertrauensmann*). They must also be members of the German Labor Front and offer the necessary guaranties that they will at any time be ready "to defend the National State."

Every year, in March, the head of the enterprise, together with the factory Nazi party cell (N.S.B.O.), draws up a list of candidates to the Work Council, taken from his employees who comply with the conditions set forth in the law. This list can be adopted or rejected in toto by the employees in secret vote only. If the list is rejected, the required number of members will be appointed by the Labor Trustee.

Labor Trustees

Labor Trustees, as direct representatives or commissioners of the central government in all labor matters, were already appointed in May, 1933, for the thirteen districts into which all Germany was subdivided for this purpose. They have, during the first year of Nazi rule in Germany, exercised practically dictatorial powers in regulating labor conditions and especially wages. The new law is to define more clearly and precisely their functions. Their main duty is to safeguard the maintenance of industrial peace. In order to fulfill this task they have to watch over the composition and procedure of the Work Councils and make the necessary decisions in case of conflicts arising in these Councils between employers and employees. The Labor Trustees have, as already indicated, to appoint the members of these Councils in case the list submitted by the employer is rejected by his staff. In case the Work Council appeals to the Trustee against decisions taken by the employer in regard to general conditions of work, he has to examine the matter and, if necessary, make the decisions himself. One of the functions of the Labor Trustee which is likely to be of particular importance in practice is to prevent or postpone mass dismissals of employees by industrial enterprises. These latter have to advise the Labor Trustee at least four weeks in advance of any mass dismissals they may contemplate. These four weeks may be prolonged by the Labor Trustee to two months, and simultaneously he may take the necessary steps in order to spread work in the meantime.

Any person, whether employer or employee, who violates directions and regulations issued by the Trustee can be sentenced to a fine or, in more serious cases, to imprisonment.

Fixation of Wages

As a matter of principle, the fixation of current wage scales is a privilege of the employer or "leader" of the enterprise. The new Labor Code thus emphatically denies the old wage agreements which were negotiated for whole districts and branches of industry by unions of employers and employees. However, by a special provision of the law, wage scales, now in force in Germany by virtue of such agreements, are to remain in force till April 30, 1934, when the new law becomes operative in its entirety.

The fixation of wage rates by the employer can either be included in the general work regulation (*Betriebsordnung*) or may be the subject of a special regulation. These regulations are legally binding for all employees. However, the Labor Trustee is authorized to fix minimum wages for his district. As already indicated, it is impossible to say from the outset which of these two methods will prevail, i.e., that of fixing wage rates individually for each enterprise by its "leader," which will unavoidably result in a great variety of wage scales within the same industry, or that of uniform fixation of minimum wages by the Labor Trustee. This will in the long run depend entirely on the spirit in which the law is administered and on the frequency of appeals by employees against the fixation of wages by their employers.

Protection Against Dismissal

In one rather important respect the new Labor Code provides additional protection to workers—that against dismissal by the employers. In enterprises with a total number of workmen exceeding ten, an employee or worker who has been employed for more than one year and who has been given notice of dismissal by the employer may sue the latter for withdrawal of the notice in case the dismissal can be considered as an unjustified hardship or if it is not warranted by the situation of the enterprise.

If the court rules that the notice should be withdrawn, it

must also fix the amount of the indemnity in case the employer should not agree to rescind the notice. The employer will then have the option either to re-employ the dismissed worker or to pay the indemnity fixed by the court. This indemnity, which must be proportionate to the period of time the workman has been employed, should not, however, exceed one-third of his total earnings during the last year.

"Social Honor" Courts

The authors of the new law attribute special importance to these new courts, which will have to guarantee that all parties concerned, namely, employers and employees, will base their actions on the high ideal of "social honor." This alone would, in their opinion, justify the wide rights and privileges granted to industrial leaders under the new law.

The "courts of honor" are to be composed of a judge acting as chairman, and of two members—a head of a concern and a member of a Work Council, namely, an employee. The members are to be chosen by the chairman from lists presented by the German Labor Front.

All offenses against social obligations imposed by the new "Work Community" are considered as a breach against "social honor" and are subject to the jurisdiction of the new courts. In particular, any misuse of his "position of power" by the employer in order to exploit his workers will be punishable as a breach of the "social honor" of his followers. A similar breach of "social honor" is constituted when employees unduly interfere with the running of the business, and thus violate the privileges of their industrial leader. Furthermore, the disclosure of production secrets to competitors by members of the staff is considered as a specially heavy offense against "social honor."

The punishments which the "court of honor" can impose consist of reprimands, fines up to ten thousand marks, denial of the ability of an employer to exercise his function as an industrial leader, and the dismissal of employees. Obviously, this right of the "court of honor" virtually to depose the head of a concern, who, in its opinion, has made himself guilty of a breach of "social honor" is one of the most far-reaching though vague provisions of the law. The extent to which the courts will actually avail themselves of this legal possibility will, as already indicated, to a large extent determine the actual influence which the code will have on industrial conditions in general.

Influence of State and Party

Although the new Labor Code considers it one of its main objectives to free the employer of all restrictions imposed upon him by law and by labor unions under the old régime, and thus to restore his freedom of action as a real "industrial leader" with all privileges and responsibilities, it is necessary to point out that the State and the ruling party are able to influence in many ways not only the actual administration of the law, but also the performance of his functions by the head of an enterprise himself. This applies in particular to the election of the Work Council, where the list of the employers' candidates has to be O.K.'d by the Nazi factory cell, i.e., an organ of the party. If the list is rejected by the employees, the members of the Council are appointed by the Labor Trustee, an official of the Federal Labor Ministry with dictatorial powers. Furthermore, all employees or workmen elected or appointed to the Work Council must belong to the German Labor Front, also an organization controlled by the party, which has taken the place of the former trade unions. Finally, the members of the courts of honor also can be drawn only from lists of candidates presented by the Labor Front.

17

INDUSTRY UNDER THE NAZIS

Berlin, February 8, 1934

No DOUBT, the leaders of the National Socialist movement in Germany are intensely patriotic and sincere in their efforts to improve every phase of the country's activities. Unfortunately, almost all of them are inexperienced, not to say ignorant, and display in their statements and actions a considerable amount of infantilism. They are simply not adult, experienced men of the world. It seems likely that in the long run many of their policies adopted in ignorance will lead to quite different results than those contemplated. An example of this lies in the extreme protectionism with which they are treating the machinery industry.

The responsible government officials are taking the position that Germany, being one of the leading machinery producers and exporters of the world and possessing a well-organized industry and splendid scientific equipment, should be completely self-supporting in machinery and technical equipment. Accordingly, they are refusing to grant foreign exchange for the importation of almost all foreign products in these fields. Recently a representative of an American company stated that sixty American winding machines ordered by the Glanzstoff concern are still lying in Antwerp and cannot be imported into Germany for lack of foreign-exchange permits. This is in spite of the fact that their installation is considered absolutely necessary in order that Glanzstoff may supply Australian orders for artificial silk which it now has on hand to the extent of four hundred thousand marks. It was even suggested that the British firm of Courtaulds, which is interested in Glanzstoff, together with the Australian importers of the German artificial silk, should make a present of the American machines to Glanzstoff in order that the contract be concluded. The Glanzstoff officials, however, were afraid to accept the foreign machines, even as a present, since they felt that this would lead to a very close scrutiny of their books by government officials and put them in a suspect position.

On some occasions, however, a certain number of foreign machines have got in. The Gute Hoffnung Huette has just obtained a few forging machines from Great Britain which were absolutely necessary in order to carry out a contract for supplying two million marks' worth of steel products for British customers. After long negotiations the government here agreed to allow the imported machinery to be set off against part of the steel exports.

Yesterday, one of the largest machinery dealers and importers of Germany was describing to me the situation in the machine-tool industry. He stated that he has been importing and distributing annually from fifteen to twenty American high-speed machine tools designed to make a certain automobile part; but he estimates that six of these machines a year would be enough to cover all the requirements of the German automobile industry if they were used full time. The authorities here have refused to give any more foreign exchange for the importation of these machines and are making plans for their manufacture in Germany. There is not even the remotest chance that such an industry could pay its way or earn even a respectable fraction of the amount invested. In the case of the winding machines just mentioned, the German authorities stated that they were putting local engineers to work here to design and build machines similar to the American article which would do the necessary work. The American company tells me that they have complete patent protection and in any fair court could prevent the use of such machinery by injunction. It is believed here that important German firms are going to be heavily handicapped by the lack of necessary foreign equipment as soon as their present machines wear out.

The continued demands for cash made upon the German industry, the continuing high taxation and the enforced employment of thousands of superfluous persons, merely to keep them off the streets, is reducing the cash reserves of many important companies and forcing them to save money by a stoppage of research and laboratory work. In this way the very flower of German industrial efficiency is being slowly destroyed, although the government and the public here are blissfully ignorant of the fact and will not wake up to it until a very long period of time has passed.

In a recent talk with the chief engineer of an American tractor company, he told me that his firm has been obliged to stop using German Diesel engines and Diesel equipment, particularly high-pressure pumps which were formerly obtained from Robert Bosch of Stuttgart, because the standard of quality and precision was so poor that the products were unusable; and that the Bosch company had informed him that it was impossible for them to better their standards at the present time. Furthermore, complaints are general that the quality of

German steel, particularly high-speed steels and special alloy steels, is unsatisfactory for fine work.

But German industry is not falling behind in its laboratory and technical positions alone. The whole field of scientific endeavor here has been very drastically hemmed in by the recent political developments. Consider the restriction of free speech and the regimentation of thought along certain favorite lines, together with the vast amount of time-wasting, which is going on in the universities, in military drills and lectures on racial theory.

The Berlin *Hendelshochschule* has been practically dismantled and its chief, Professor Bonn, is now in England or America. The Market Research Institute of the Department of Agriculture has been entirely dismantled. Its chief fled to New York a few hours ahead of the S.A. It is my impression, confirmed by the statements of a number of students both German and foreign, that the universities have suffered heavily in their scientific attainments in the last year. Some students have told me that they consider their year 1933 almost entirely wasted from the standpoint of study and research.

Hitler refers to this fact in his speech to the students on February 7, where he states that in these times of racial crisis individual careers must be sacrificed to the future of the German race. A careful perusal of his speech, which was supposed to contain the principles governing the new National Organization of University Students, reveals the fact that the man is suffering from almost insane delusions regarding the importance of racial matters. He is building his whole political and social philosophy upon a complex of half-baked, unscientific and vague notions which have never even been clearly defined by anyone, let alone been proved by any scientific tests whatever. What must be the mental state of German university students whose whole philosophy of life is based upon this vague and undigested mess? One of Hitler's statements, as nearly as it can be stated in clear language which has any definite meaning, is that the communist movement with its slogan "Workers of the World! Unite!" is primarily a racial movement. Apparently he believes that in most of the white nations several races are present and that the working class in the various nations is all made up of, more or less, the same race. What that race is, he does not say. By uniting all these workers internationally, a racial front is to be built which is directed against the Nordic race. The duty of German university students is, therefore, to hold fast to Nordic principles and bind the other racial elements in Germany, particularly the working classes, to the Nordic chariot, and especially to see to it that the Jews are not allowed to alienate these other races away from their natural and God-given Nordic leaders. This is the substance of Hitler's principles as laid down for the guidance of the German university world.

He emphasizes that membership in the Nordic race is not to be determined or inferred from external appearances, i.e., stature, color of hair or eyes, or physical characteristics. He declares that the actions of the individual and his character are the best indication of what race he really belongs to. This is a new definition of race and somewhat revises the existing conceptions of the National Socialist party. It would seem that this definition renders any distinction based upon race quite meaningless, but nevertheless Hitler insists that race is still all-important, although seemingly neither he nor anyone else can exactly define what it is.

With the start of 1934, careful observers could begin to see the emergence of Hitler's long-range military plans. The memorandum which follows was prepared for the American Embassy in Berlin. A portion of this chapter has already been published in Peace and War, *the official White Book.* . . .

18

BUSINESS RELATIONS WITH THE
UNITED STATES

Berlin, April 17, 1934

THE NATIONAL SOCIALIST GOVERNMENT in Germany is now appealing to the United States government for financial assistance with the alleged object of maintaining imports of American raw materials, but with the more important object in mind of continuing the National Socialist régime in power. To understand the present situation in Germany, it is necessary to examine briefly the purposes and policies of National Socialism.

The fundamental purpose is to secure a greater share of the world's future for the Germans, the expansion of German territory and growth of the German race until it constitutes the largest and most powerful nation in the world, and ultimately, according to some Nazi leaders, until it dominates the entire globe.

The German people, suffering from a traditional inferiority

complex, smarting from their defeat in the war and the indignities of the post-war period, disillusioned in their hopes of a speedy return to prosperity along traditional lines, inflamed by irresponsible demagogic slogans and flattered by the statement that their German racial inheritance gives them inherent superior rights over other peoples, have to a large measure adopted the National Socialist point of view.

Economic Aims

There are two other purposes subsidiary to the main purpose. Germany is to be made the economic center of a self-sustaining territorial bloc whose dependent nations in Central and Eastern Europe will look to Berlin for leadership. This bloc is to be so constituted that it can defy wartime blockade and be large enough to give the peoples in it the benefit of free trade now enjoyed by the forty-eight American states. In accordance with this purpose, an agricultural self-sufficiency program has been adopted, foreign foodstuffs are being rigorously excluded or the imported supply secured in increasing quantities from Central and Southeastern Europe. A hereditary peasantry has been set up, firmly attached to the soil through the prohibition of the sale or mortgaging of the peasant's land or crops. An increasing number of commodities have been placed under government monopolies with fixed prices to consumers and producers. The principle of the *Numerus Clausus*, or fixed number of persons engaged in any occupation, has been increasingly adopted. The National Socialist conception of the correct or government-fixed price instead of the price fixed by supply and demand has been introduced.

Social Aims

The second subsidiary purpose is the welding of all individuals in the present and future Greater Germany into a homogeneous racial family, gladly obedient to the will of its leader, with class and cultural differences inside the country eliminated, but a sharp line drawn between Germans and the foreign world outside. In carrying out this purpose, the Jews are to be entirely eliminated, the Slavic or Eastern elements in the population to be minimized and eventually bred out of the race. A national religion is in process of organization; trade unions, political parties and all social, political, cultural, trade or other organizations not affiliated with the National Socialist party have been abolished; the individual's rights have been largely taken away. In the future, the nation is to count for everything, the individual for nothing. Germany is to engage in a gigantic struggle with the rest of the world to grow at the expense of its neighbors. The German population owes the nation the patriotic duty of supporting it and bringing forward all necessary sacrifices to reach the common goal.

Retention of Power

To these long-distance objectives must be added the fourth and most important purpose of all, namely, to retain control at all costs. The National Socialist party may compromise on distant objectives, if necessary, but cannot compromise on a question of retaining its absolute hold on the German people. This control has been gained by making most irresponsible and extravagant promises; by the studied use of the press, the radio, public meetings, parades, flags, uniforms, and all methods of working on popular psychology, and finally by the use of force. This control, once lost, could never be regained. It is absolutely necessary for the party to continue to make a show of success and to keep popular enthusiasm and fanaticism alive. There must be no open criticism or grumbling; even discussion of the future form of the State, the form in which industry is to be organized, or the laws regarding the hereditary peasantry, is prohibited. Since the German public is politically inept and unusually docile, the Nazi movement has been able to dominate the situation for the past year, but the hard facts of the economic situation are beginning to be felt by the more intelligent Germans, particularly the bankers, businessmen, professional men and persons who are in touch with the outside world.

The Government Employment Program

In order to obtain power, the Nazis promised to cure the unemployment problem. They have already reduced unemployment from about six million to less than three million, partly by a policy of government expenditure for construction, by sharing jobs, by removing women from the labor market, and by creating employment in the manufacture of uniforms, military equipment, furniture for couples subsidized with government dowries. Government expenditures for public works are set at about six billion marks. Of this amount, one and a half billion has already been expended. The government pays in short-term Treasury bills which are discounted by the banks, and of which about a billion marks remain in the banks at the present time under government pressure to retain them there. One half-billion marks have already been rediscounted by the Reichsbank. Eventually, the entire amount must be shouldered by the Reichsbank, creating credit inflation. German bankers in favor of this plan feel that action of this kind was absolutely necessary; they hope that recovery of world business will come along and catch up with the artificial stimulation of domestic business now well started under government borrowing, and that in this way Germany can anticipate world recovery by a year or two. At the worst, they feel it is unimportant whether national bankruptcy takes place at a figure of one billion or ten billion marks. In the meantime, the population is being fed and given hope; in other words, this policy is a gigantic gamble on the date and the extent of world economic recovery and the extent to which Germany can participate in it.

The German Budget

The ordinary budget aside from emergency unemployment expenditure is theoretically balanced at six thousand four hundred and fifty-eight million marks. Tax receipts are estimated at one hundred and thirty-three million less than last year. New sources of tax revenue cannot be found because the social changes in Germany (shifting wealth to a large number of party members and former unemployed) results in a smaller amount of taxable property and income remaining in possession of persons who can be taxed. Government receipts also include two hundred and twenty million marks from the sale of preferred shares of the Federal Railroads, three hundred million marks from the sale of other assets held by the government, and finally two hundred and seventy million marks to be borrowed by a public loan. The sinking fund of one hundred million marks traditionally set aside to reduce the floating debt has been abandoned. On the expenditure side, the government has increased expenditures for military purposes by seven hundred million marks, including three hundred and twenty-three million for the army and navy, one hundred and thirty million for aviation and two hundred and fifty million for the Nazi Storm Detachments and Labor Service. Expenditures also show a reduction of three hundred and eighty million marks for unemployment doles, which is set off against the six billion being spent for creation of new employment. In other words, the German government, while dangerously inflating the money market by creating employment on short-term borrowing, is heavily expanding its military preparations and pawning its fixed assets.

Foreign Debts

The German government is now engaged in negotiations with its long-term creditors in the hope of stopping payment of interest and amortization on its long-term and medium-term debt, which amounts roughly to ten billion marks. About one billion dollars of long-term bonds are held in the United States. Germany is now entering a plea of bankruptcy in gold and foreign exchange, the Reichsbank's reserves amounting to two hundred and forty-five million marks on March 28, 1934, or six and seven-tenths per cent of the note circulation. It is quite clear that the Germans have now reached the stage where they can no longer pay interest on their short-term commercial debt, on their long-term bonds, and still import their necessary raw materials. The National Socialist movement has very decidedly helped in bringing about this state of things. Before the party came into power, in December, 1932, Germany was finally relieved of her reparations burden. The movement of foreign capital out of the country which brought about the bank and foreign-exchange crisis of July, 1931, and which had resulted in the imposition of foreign-exchange restrictions, began in the fall of 1930 in reaction to the National Socialist victory in the elections in September that year, when the party for the first time returned one hundred and seven deputies to the Reichstag as compared with only a handful before. It was the fear of a Nazi government and its campaign of hate against Jewish and foreign capital that drove money out of the country. This movement became cumulative and has finally resulted in an almost complete breakdown of German business with the outside world.

Short-term Debts

Germany's short-term obligations, largely commercial acceptances, are regulated by the Standstill Agreement of February, 1933. The total amount of short-term foreign indebtedness is about six billion marks. Short-term credits under the Standstill Agreement amount now to less than two and a half billion marks, of which about half represent commercial acceptances. The bulk of these are in the hands of American banks. Interest rates are four and one-half to five per cent. Some American banking representatives have frankly expressed their hope that the United States government might grant credits to Germany which would enable their German debtors to pay off these short-term credits so that the American banks could retire from a field which has been profitable but which they feel is becoming too risky at the present time.

Undoubtedly, the short-term commercial creditors are in a position much preferable to that of the holders of long-term bonds. These bonds are owned by thousands of individual holders, mostly in the United States, who are at a disadvantage in negotiating with the German government.

Repatriation of Bonds

In the last two years, Dr. Schacht and his colleagues have from time to time uttered sharp warnings about the German situation, and these have caused German bond prices in the United States to fall heavily. On the basis of these low prices and assisted by the depreciation of the dollar, the Germans have been doing a lively business in repatriating bonds into Germany to an extent, admitted by the Reichsbank, of seven hundred and eighty-one million marks at the end of last year, but estimated by American bankers as considerably more. In other words, the Germans by injuring their credit abroad have been able to buy back their bonds at twenty-five cents on the dollar in large quantities, and now, having used up their foreign exchange in this manner, confront us with the fact that they are unable to go on paying interest on the remainder of the bonds. It should be remembered that at the time these bonds were issued the German government had instituted a *Beratungsstelle,* or Consulting Office, which passed upon the purposes for which loans could be made abroad and the extent to which this was desirable, and was empowered to refuse to permit loans at the government's discretion.

Foreign Exchange

The Reichsbank's gold and foreign-exchange holdings of March 28, 1934, are set at two hundred and forty-five million marks, compared with three hundred and ninety-five million on January first, 1934. The foreign-exchange situation is particularly acute in view of the declining volume of Germany's exports:

December, 1933

Exports	424,000,000	marks
Imports	374,000,000	marks
Gain	50,000,000	marks

January, 1934

Exports	350,000,000	marks
Imports	372,000,000	marks
Loss	22,000,000	marks

February, 1934

Exports	334,000,000	marks
Imports	378,000,000	marks
Loss	44,000,000	marks

German exports are continually falling in view of the high domestic price level, the policy of the National Socialist party to maintain or increase wage rates and the maintenance of gold parity of the mark. Furthermore, the boycott of German goods abroad is being felt with increasing severity. It is easy to boycott goods when the price is high.

In the last few years, Germany has been meeting the interest on her foreign indebtedness by her surplus of exports over imports, which amounted to one billion seventy-three million marks in 1932 or an average of eighty-nine million marks per month; six hundred and sixty-seven million in 1933 or an average of fifty-five million marks per month. This year, the balance is the other way. Furthermore, as pointed out by Dr. Schacht, the export figures include a large amount of business, possibly up to one hundred million marks per month, which is financed by the use of scrip and blocked marks. This scrip is the untransferable portion of interest on German bonds due to foreigners and is sold at a varying discount here but credited to exporters at full value. The discount in 1933 was fifty per cent, which was lowered to thirty-three per cent in January and in the next few days will probably be placed upon a fluctuating basis. Blocked marks are marks owned in Germany by foreigners and untransferable into foreign exchange at their face value. They can be traded in at varying discounts, at the present time between thirty and forty per cent. In other words, perhaps one hundred million marks per month of present German exports were financed through these methods, so that on this one hundred million marks of foreign business Germany actually received in foreign exchange only sixty per cent of the invoice value of the goods.

Soviet Payments

On the other hand, Dr. Schacht has omitted to mention that the import figures do not all represent a claim on foreign exchange. Imports from Russia are not paid for in foreign exchange but are credited against the Soviet indebtedness to Germany, which still amounts to about seven hundred and fifty million marks. Of this amount, approximately six hundred million marks were due in 1934. Some of this has been prolonged into subsequent years by an agreement just signed with the Russians; but it seems clear that the Germans can count upon receipts of goods, foreign exchange and gold, amounting to perhaps four hundred million marks from Russia this year, for which they do not have to pay anything.

In view of Dr. Schacht's performances in past negotiations, it is not too much to suggest that after the coming transfer conference this month, when Germany has made the best possible deal with Western creditors and the Reichsbank's position has been allowed to drop to an alarming figure, new payments from Russia will be quickly added to the credit side of the ledger of the Reichsbank and Dr. Schacht will point out to his German public the increasing soundness of the Reichsbank, the stability of the mark and the sound financial position of the country for carrying out its extensive program of domestic construction.

Foreign-exchange Control

Ever since the financial crisis of July, 1931, Germany has had a very strict foreign-exchange control. Importers of foreign products who were in business before that date were allowed monthly quotas of foreign exchange to be used in payment of imports. This quota was originally set at fifty per cent of the business which the existing import firms had been doing in previous years. By the beginning of 1934, importers were only allowed fifty per cent of their quota per month as a maximum. This amount was cut in March to forty-five per cent and in April to thirty-five per cent, or, more accurately, seventeen and one-half per cent of the foreign-exchange requirements of German importers in 1930. It should be emphasized that this seventeen and one-half per cent is a maximum figure. For many dispensable items, even this amount is not allowed.

The policy of the Reichsbank and the Ministry of Economics which administers these foreign-exchange regulations has been to conduct Germany's foreign trade on a foreign-exchange basis, i.e., not to send marks out of the country, in order to prevent any business going on in mark quotations abroad which might impair the stability of the mark. In the last few days, foreign-exchange authorities have apparently altered their system, and in some cases are refusing to grant dollar exchange here but are allowing importers to sell mark drafts in New York. The result has been a weakness of the mark in New York. It is not too much to suggest that this show of weakness has been deliberately maneuvered at this time in order to bring home to the United States the perilous financial situation in Germany and put additional pressure upon us for financial assistance.

General Methods of Import Control

In addition to the regulations for foreign-exchange quotas, which hold down German imports as a whole to a maximum of seventeen and one-half per cent of pre-crisis years, a series of restrictive regulations have been put into effect which are now threatening to bring Germany's foreign trade almost to a complete standstill. The purpose of these regulations is apparently, first, to protect Germany's supplies of foreign exchange, secondly, to render the country self-sufficient in food products and other essential items (this has primarily a political and military significance rather than a merely economic one), thirdly, to use these regulations as a bargaining weapon with foreign countries, and fourthly, to give the German government control over essential commodities. This is done partly to remove business from Jewish hands, partly to allocate business inside the country according to the government's desires; possibly to build up stocks of necessary war materials in safe hands, and finally to assist the government in substituting fixed prices and monopoly control instead of the free movement of commodities regulated by supply-and-demand, which is contrary to National Socialist economic theory.

Import Quota System

In the place of general most-favored-nation commercial treaties, of which Germany was a leading exponent several years ago, the German government started recently to make special reciprocal commercial treaties with neighboring countries, setting up import quotas for specified products or special quotas at lowered conventional tariff rates. This policy was initiated in the treaties with Finland, Sweden and Denmark as far back as 1930, covering such items as cattle, butter and timber. From this point on the growth of the quota system has been rapid until now it embraces a wide variety of products and the principle has been incorporated into commercial treaties with many foreign countries, particularly Germany's near neighbors.

Monopolies

Since the advent of the National Socialist régime, a group of government monopolies of specified products has been instituted. These include both imported and domestic goods, and force all business through the hands of the government's buying and selling agencies at fixed prices. In the beginning, this system was confined to grain, principally wheat, rye and corn. Later on, it extended to butter, margarine, lard, vegetable oils and edible fats, cheese, eggs and milk. More recently, it has included cotton, wool, other textile fabrics, copper and other nonferrous metals, hides and skins, abrasives, animal products, and a growing list of other commodities. Little information is made public in Germany about this new development, although in the course of time it must become generally known.

The monopoly authorities operate under the existing commodity quotas now incorporated in Germany's commercial treaties with foreign countries, but many of these quotas are secret. Nationals of one country are kept in the dark as to what the other foreign countries are getting. There is no appeal from the decisions of the monopolies, which can refuse to purchase and make free use of their power to condemn imported shipments as not up to standard. To show how this system works, take the case of an importer of butter in Germany. He must first of all possess a monthly quota of foreign exchange or else he cannot pay for his imported supplies. Next he must import from some country which has a quota, paying the high tariff rates of seventy-five marks per one hundred kilograms. In addition to this, he must pay equalization fees set up by the monopoly and varying from month to month. In fact, the amount of butter quotas from different countries and the amount of the equalization fee for the current month are often not known until the month is more than half over. The equalization fees on butter are now eighty-two marks per one hundred kilograms over and above the tariff rates. Furthermore, he must pay certain monopoly fees for administrative costs of the monopoly and for other purposes; for example, the egg monopoly recently informed all Aryan egg dealers that they could register as dealers under the monopoly upon payment of a fee of one thousand marks. It developed that this fee was to be used to set up in business various National Socialist egg merchants to take the place of existing Jewish houses, which will be entirely excluded from the egg business in the future.

146

Finally, the importer has no guaranty that the monopoly will allow his product to be sold. His application may be refused and he has no redress. At the present time new monopolies, new quota arrangements, new fees are set up so fast that no one even in the German government can know what products are covered and what, in fact, the regulations are. The Agricultural Ministry in particular is secretive and refuses to tell other ministries in the German government what plans it is undertaking. The entire action is extremely arbitrary and destructive. At the present time, until some of these new monopolies can be set up, purchase of foreign products has been entirely prohibited. This applies at the present time to cotton, wool, other textile fibers, hides and skins, and copper. It is believed here that this prohibition is likely to be extended soon to petroleum, coffee and certain other items.

The Export Situation

Germany's exports have in the last few months been falling even faster than imports. This was due at the beginning of the present year principally to the high prices of German goods. For the most part, Germany exports a wide range of highly manufactured articles. She has few raw materials or food products to sell. In the beginning of the world depression, Germany had an advantage because prices of raw materials were falling faster than those of finished goods. This gave Germany an export advantage in 1930, 1931 and 1932. This advantage is being changed to a disadvantage now as world prices of raw materials, which Germany must import, are rising and the demand for finished goods is low. Most of Germany's finished exports are fairly low in quality; for example, hardware, textiles, toys, glassware, pottery, chemicals, machinery, and are competed with by products of many other foreign countries. They are the sort of goods sold in bazaars of Asia and Africa or in the ten-cent stores and department-store basements in the United States. Their price must be low in order to attract business. On the contrary, German domestic and export prices are now high and are tending to rise rather than fall. Not only does Germany retain the mark at nominal parity, but wage levels have been maintained and may even be increased under the National Socialist movement, which is essentially a proletarian movement at heart. German business firms not only have to pay high taxes but are forced to increase their number of employees under Nazi pressure whether or not this is justified by current orders. Furthermore, they are under severe pressure to make continuous contributions to the Nazi funds, their domestic turnover is low and they are simply unable to quote low export prices.

Export Subsidies

The German government has attempted to assist exports by allowing exporters to purchase scrip, blocked marks or German bonds abroad at the heavy discount already described, and to turn these in in Germany at a higher figure. These methods have assisted exports considerably, but too much cannot be expected from them. The method of export subsidies through bond repatriation comes to an end as soon as German capital inside the country is no longer available to redeem bonds, and German funds which have fled to foreign countries can no longer be induced back through the profit held out in this way, a profit which has been from forty to fifty per cent recently. It is evident now that the German financial situation is so serious that what remains of German capital abroad can no longer be induced to come back, no matter what the nominal rate of profit in marks may be, while a considerable amount of these funds represents Jewish capital which is afraid to come back under any circumstances.

The method of subsidizing exports through the use of scrip and blocked marks is limited in extent to the amount of scrip and blocked marks which are available. Scrip represents interest payments on Germany's long-term debt and the total amount is small compared with former foreign trade figures. It is estimated by Dr. Schacht that two hundred million marks of exports were financed through scrip and blocked marks in the five months ended November, 1933, and since then an average of one hundred million marks per month. The amount of business which can be done in this way is not enough by itself to maintain existing export trade, nor is it enough to be a serious threat to other exporting nations.

You Can't Do Business With Hitler

It is particularly difficult for the United States to come to any commercial agreement with Germany regarding reciprocal exchange of merchandise. Germany begins by shutting out practically all our food products. This, as has previously been stated, is not to protect the foreign-exchange situation but is part of the economic program of self-sufficiency adopted primarily for military reasons. Germany, however, needs American cotton, copper, petroleum and other raw materials. These cannot be produced inside the country and there are no real substitutes available in adequate amounts at the present time, although the Germans are making great efforts to meet this situation.

But on the American side there is little that Germany has to sell for which we can offer an increasing market. There is the one item of potash, which we need in large quantities and for which we can guarantee future business. But nearly all the rest of Germany's sales to the United States are comprised of a multitude of small manufactured articles, none of which are of staple character, many of which are subject to changes in style and popular taste. It is impossible for us to guarantee to increase the sale of German cotton stockings and gloves, crockery, glass beads, cameras, mouth organs or penknives. The utmost we can do is to lower or remove the tariff on such articles. Even then, at present German prices there is not much of this stuff which would find an active market in the United States. Under the present régime, the standards of quality in Germany are sinking. There is little incentive for the investment of money in new designs and new products, and it looks as if under the Nazi system of fixed prices and controlled business German-manufactured goods will be increasingly unable to compete in the highly critical American market.

Difficulties of Dealing With Germany

The present period, April, 1934, is a particularly difficult one in which to take up the settlement of commercial questions between Germany and the United States. For one thing, the monopoly system in Germany with its fixed prices, allocation of supplies and government-controlled business has not yet been in action long enough to see how it will work. The grain monopoly has not yet had a full year of operation, the same is true of the fat monopoly, and as for the others, they have only been created in the last few days and have not yet worked out their own methods. It will take some period of time before it will become evident how much American cotton and other products Germany can and will actually buy under this system. Certainly, in the case of cotton, German mills cannot easily scrap their existing machinery, which is suited to American cotton lengths, and go over to Indian cotton, as they are reported in the newspapers to be planning.

It is still too early for anyone to say how the fat monopoly will work out. The German import quota for foreign lard was set some time in March at a figure of forty per cent of the average for the last three years, thus heavily cutting down American sales. This is our second most important export item to Germany, only exceeded by cotton, but the forty-per-cent quota adopted in March is already out of date in mid-April. The fat authorities have not been able to decide what, if any, quota of foreign lard they could allow in April, and so far none has been allowed in during the second month of the quota's operation, although the month is half gone. The forty-per-cent quota was originally set up for an entire year. This shows how rapidly conditions are changing in Germany now. Any trade agreement which the United States makes with Germany, if it is to have any value over a period of years, can only be made when things here have settled down.

Probable Fall in the Mark

Another reason why commercial negotiations with Germany now are of questionable value is the fact that the German currency is being maintained at an artificially high gold parity which has no relation to its real value or to the actual economic situation of Germany and the rest of the world today. The absurdly high value of the mark can only be maintained by the most stringent currency restrictions and prevention of any free movement of capital out of Germany. It is clear that Germany cannot abandon her restrictions until the mark is put at a natural and reasonable value, that is, devalued to at least half of its present figure. The German government for reasons of its own prestige and fear of loss of confidence by its own population hesitates to take this painful but necessary step. However, the facts of the situation will tell in the long run and Germany must devaluate the mark some day. Only after this happens can satisfactory long-term commercial negotiations with the United States be made.

Nazi Unreliability

There also remain other reasons why Americans who are long resident in Germany and familiar with the situation are not hopeful that much can be accomplished by commercial negotiations between the United States and Germany. The present German government, as compared with other German governments in the past, is conspicuous for its lack of truthfulness, reliability and spirit of fair dealing. Nazi psychology appears to include a feeling that Germany has been so ill-treated by other countries that any underhanded methods are justified in dealing with foreigners. Hitler even publicly advocates in his well-known book *Mein Kampf* the use of lying and deception in a good cause. The National Socialist movement is notorious for its contempt of the elementary principles of justice and its failure to recognize the rights of the individual, whether foreign or German. We can be sure that any bargain or agreement we make with the National Socialists will be kept by them only to such an extent and so long as they deem it advantageous.

Furthermore, any agreement made with the German government binds only the government itself and not the all-powerful National Socialist party. Party organization parallels the government structure; its regulations have the force of law inside Germany but remain purely unofficial. A few days ago, the party industry leader, Kessler, issued an order to all manufacturers of cigarettes to buy no more Bulgarian tobacco in view of certain differences between the German and Bulgarian governments. This order will be implicitly obeyed, but there is nothing the Bulgarians can do about it. A power of this kind held in reserve makes official agreements between Germany and the foreign world illusory. Action of this kind may be politely deplored by the German government, but it persists nevertheless.

For example, American exporters of farm machinery, automobiles, office equipment, machine tools and other items, whose origin is conspicuous and which can always be identified as American, are finding that it is getting more difficult every day to sell goods in Germany because over and above all other difficulties German purchasers are simply afraid to buy these articles and are frank in saying so. For example, most German farmers do not dare to buy and use an American tractor or harvester at this time, as they would be immediately known as lukewarm nationalists and be subject to reprisals from neighbors in all sorts of ways. Similarly, local Nazi organizations have passed resolutions stating their belief that it was improper for certain of their members to drive American automobiles. These resolutions have the effect of law. No one dares defy the party inside Germany these days. Such action against foreign products is not taken by the German government, or as a rule it does not come from the central national organization of the party but from its local branches. It is, nevertheless, completely effective. How can we hope to enter into fruitful negotiations with Germany as long as this spirit persists?

American Loans to Germany

The most immediate question of the moment between Germany and the United States is the attitude which we must adopt in response to the Germans' desire for financial assistance. We can take one of three courses: first, either refuse to give any assistance either in the form of raw-material credits, government loans or the assumption of Germany's long-term debt to American investors. This course of action leaves all our existing investments in Germany in an insecure position but does not prevent our chipping away a little here and there as opportunity offers. This is the course pursued by most American banks and business firms here. They are seeking to reduce their existing investments, making only small future commitments and attempting to hold on until conditions change. It is seriously to be doubted that Germany will be able to get along without our raw materials. Germany certainly needs them more than we need the German market. Any raw-material credits which Germany requests will be for such supplies as would be imported anyway, for example, cotton. If American credits are to be given to our exporting firms to do additional business in Germany, they should be confined to those which the Germans have already ceased buying or have greatly restricted. This might mean additional trade which we would not otherwise get. Examples are: prunes, lard, grain, packing-house products, and many other items.

The second course which the American Government can

pursue is to adopt the German proposals and give financial assistance in varying forms. As previously shown, this sort of action subjects us to the danger of losing the sums advanced and throwing good money after bad. The present position in Germany, characterized by an almost complete breakdown of financial relations with the outside world and a drastic curtailment of foreign trade, including essential raw materials on the one hand, set over against a growing expansion of government credit inside Germany and forced increase of demand by the tremendous employment program, is bound to lead to a situation before very long where the mark must be revalued and where the entire domestic program must collapse if the essential foreign raw materials and credits cannot be continued in sufficient quantities. No program which merely contemplates relieving Germany of her past financial obligations will be sufficient to prevent this economic breakdown in the future, even if past debts were entirely cleared off the slate. The present position is unsound and cannot be maintained for several years without a breakdown.

Any contributions of modest amounts which the American government might make to ease the situation would simply be lost. In order to ensure the security of our existing investments and any additional credits, there is only one course of action which could be pursued, namely, to support the existing régime in Germany by every possible means, to take off Germany's shoulders her present debt burden to the United States, to grant new credits and, when these are exhausted, still more credits, and thus virtually underwrite the entire National Socialist program with all its implications. This would please the Nazis, but would involve the United States in increasing financial commitments and eventually, unless all present signs are deceptive, in a European war.

Danger of War

The Nazis are not satisfied with the existing map of Europe. They are, at heart, belligerent and aggressive. True, they desire nothing more than a period of peace for several years in which they can gradually rearm and discipline their people. This period may be five years, ten years, or longer, but the more completely their experiments succeed the more certain is a large-scale war in Europe someday.

Germany Arming in the Air

We must bear in mind that the rearming of Germany in the air is proceeding at a rapid rate. Within a year or two, Germany will possess several thousand effective airplanes. Essential parts for these machines are now being ordered from the United States, principally crankshafts, cylinder heads, flying instruments and a few other American specialties which they cannot make as well as we can. One particular company has existing orders to equip two thousand machines at the present rate of one hundred per month, a rate which is increasing as time goes on. Other American companies are also participating in this business, as are English and other foreign firms. This air program is under the special care of Minister Goering; the necessary foreign exchange is found and regularly paid, in spite of the fact that other commodities cannot be paid for.

The S.A. is being equipped more slowly for military effectiveness. It forms a half-trained army of about three million with new recruits made available every year as the members of the *Hitler Jugend* and the *Arbeitsdienst* graduate into their ranks. This is in addition to about half a million fully trained or better-trained men, including the Reichswehr, the police, the special police and the S.S. It is perhaps too much to state that the National Socialist government is at this present time actually pursuing definite plans for aggressive war against any particular country. However, it is forging a military machine which will be equally effective for offense and defense, and it is impossible to state definitely how this organization will be used. Anyone who has lived with the Nazis for several years and studied their views must be clearly convinced that this accession of military strength to Germany will be utilized to upset the existing state of affairs in Europe, which is profoundly unsatisfactory to the National Socialist movement.

Nazis Want to Wipe Out 1918

In estimating the aims and purposes of the National Socialist movement, we must not make the mistake of putting too much reliance on public statements, designed for consumption abroad, which breathe the spirit of peace and good will and assert the intention of the government to promote the welfare of the German people and good relations with their neighbors. Nor should we imagine that the present government leaders will feel and act as we would in their circumstances, namely, think only of Germany's welfare. The real emotional drive behind the Nazi program is not so much love of their own country as dislike of other countries. The Nazis will never be content in merely promoting the welfare of the German people. They desire to be feared and envied by foreigners and to wipe out the memory of 1918 by inflicting humiliations in particular upon the French, the Poles, the Czechs and anybody else they can get their hands on.

A careful examination of Hitler's book and his public speeches reveals the fact that he cannot be considered as absolutely sane and normal on this subject. The same is true of many other Nazi leaders. They have capitalized the wounded inferiority complex of the German people and magnified their own bitter feelings into a cult of dislike against the foreign world which is past the bounds of ordinary good sense and reason. Let us repeat this fact and let it sink in: the National Socialist movement is building a tremendous military machine, physically very poorly armed, but morally aggressive and belligerent. The control of this machine lies in the hands of narrow, ignorant and unscrupulous adventurers who have been slightly touched with madness from brooding over Germany's real or imagined wrongs, as well as the slights and indignities thrown in their own individual way as they attempted to organize the movement. Power of this kind concentrated in hands like these is dangerous. The Nazis are determined to secure more power and more territory in Europe. If this is voluntarily given to them by peaceful means, well and good, but if not, they will certainly use force. That is the only meaning behind the manifold activities of the movement in Germany today.

Possibility of Internal Upset

However, it is not at all certain that the movement can be carried on in its present extreme form to a point where war becomes inevitable. As time goes on, growing weaknesses in the Nazis' position inside Germany disclose themselves. From the very beginning, the Nazis could never count upon the sympathy and support of the German upper classes. These persons, while small in number, exercise a disproportionately large influence in the direction of conservatism and moderation. They can be counted upon to act as a brake upon the radical tendencies in the National Socialist movement, but their habits of mind will never incline them to revolutionary activity against any existing government no matter how much they may dislike it.

Another and much larger class of Germans have now begun to feel and to express their disappointment and disillusionment in the Nazi program. This comprises the small businessmen, white-collar employees and the farmers. These people are beginning to feel the pinch of the Nazi economic and political program which as time goes on takes away from them their existing rights of independent action, and reduces them to merely mechanical servants of the State. The small businessman is beginning to fear the introduction of the *Numerus Clausus.* He resents the control which the government is exercising over the prices at which he may buy and sell, his relations with his employees and the public. The farmers resent being tied to the soil and the prohibition of selling or mortgaging land and crops. They are beginning to resent the fixed acreages which are prescribed for them and find that the fixed prices paid for farm products by government buyers are becoming lower while the fixed selling prices in the cities remain high, giving an increasing spread which the government is taking to itself. Nevertheless, we cannot look to this class for any more than a negative point of view. The petty bourgeoisie are not revolutionaries.

There is, however, a growing prospect that the German masses must before very long feel the pinch of high prices and low wages. The present inflationary movement, with the accompanying shortage of foreign raw materials, must result either in prohibitive high prices for many of the smaller or modest luxuries and things which in the United States would be considered necessities of life, or some kind of a severe rationing program with the use of cards and coupons. The workers have been emphatically told that their share is to be a greater one and they will not peaceably and readily accept additional privations. It is not from outside the party that this dissatisfaction will be most felt, but from the ranks of the National Socialists themselves, particularly from the S.A., which even now is considerably more radical or proletarian in its point of view than the Berlin government. Most signs point to the fact that before long the National Socialist economic program will receive some sharp criticism from within its own ranks which may lead to a substantial modification of present policies. This modification may be enough to draw the teeth of the existing rearmament plan and render Germany less of a danger to the peace of the world.

Crop Failure Would Upset Entire Program

One point to remember in this connection is the fact that Germany has had a series of bumper crops, particularly in cereals, for several years. The weather has proved favorable each spring and summer. Only because of this fact was it possible for the self-sufficiency plan in grain to succeed as it has done, but sooner or later we can expect unfavorable weather and a short crop. This may come in the present year, which already has had an abnormally warm and dry winter and spring up to date. If and when the cereal crop falls below normal, then Germany will be compelled, as often in former years, to fill out her existing requirements by imports of foreign wheat and other grain, totaling perhaps one hundred to two hundred million marks. This would raise a situation quite different from that in former bad-crop years, when comparatively small losses or gains in import figures were hardly felt in view of the size of the transactions currently going on and the availability of foreign credits. Now that foreign trade has shrunk, that the total Reichsbank reserves are only a couple of hundred million marks, a situation of this kind would bring Germany face to face with a shortage of food and no cash or credit to purchase outside supplies. This might put the National Socialist government in quite a different state of mind.

United States' Attitude

The United States government should take the following attitude toward the situation in Germany:

1. We should not give financial assistance either in the form of public funds or encouragement to private firms to extend greater credits to Germany at this time.

2. We should not initiate trade negotiations at this time. When conditions in Germany are changing so rapidly we should wait, if possible, until there is a better prospect for a long-term settlement and until we can be better assured that the German government can and will carry out its part of the agreement.

3. If the German government denounces the existing commercial treaty, which expires in October, 1935, we may have to negotiate a new treaty. We should, however, postpone this action until well into 1935, if possible. The new treaty must probably include reciprocal agreements for the admission of specific products into the respective countries under favorable terms. We must be careful to include such items of existing American exports as are now especially handicapped in Germany. We need not be unduly alarmed at the possibility

of Germany stopping her takings of cotton and certain other essential raw materials, nor should we pay too much for the privilege of continuing this business. For the most part it will be continued under any circumstances. We should endeavor to make tariff concessions on certain German products in the United States, to enable Germany to liquidate additional imports of American products.

4. We should advise American firms to reduce their outstanding commitments in Germany, when possible.

5. We should protest vigorously against violations of our existing commercial treaty or any other unfair treatment of American nationals, American products or American investments in Germany.

In order to spare the reader, only a few more reports of early Nazi days are included. They are now more widely spaced in time and are just enough to give an indication of how events were moving in Germany. . . .

19

SIDELIGHTS ON THE SITUATION

Berlin, April 27, 1934

AN IMPORTANT DEVELOPMENT in the National Socialist movement in Germany lies in the growing efforts of members of the party to cash in on their membership in some way or other. An interesting example of this is the organization of the SAGT, or self-help organization, to which only National Socialists can belong. All members are entitled when making retail purchases to utter the magic password *Sagt* in shops which are affiliated with the movement. This entitles them to receive a special receipt showing the amount of their purchase and the date. These receipts are to be kept and turned in in an envelope to the Nazi block leader at the end of the month. He, in turn, turns them all back to the retailers who then give a cash refund based on the amount of the purchases in their shops during the month. This is divided proportionately among the buyers. Presumably the National Socialist party also gets a rake-off. In this way party members are enabled to buy more cheaply than other classes of the population.

The official *Voelkischer Beobachter* carries today a picture of a mother's card of honor which is to be carried by the mothers of one or more children in good standing in the party. This entitles them to a special discount on purchases in shops, excluding department stores and Jewish-owned establishments, which are also excluded from the *Sagt* arrangement.

Duty-performance Card

In the districts of South Hanover and Brunswick, the National Socialist leaders have introduced a new duty-performance card, which comprises ten points which must be earned within a period of four months. The ten points have been so arranged that any person is supposed to be able to complete them. According to the dispatch in the *Frankfurter Zeitung,* dated March 26, the completion of these ten points is compulsory in the district for all persons over fifteen years of age. The ten points are earned in the following way. Any young person who voluntarily gives up his job in favor of a married unemployed candidate can earn ten points at once, if he then goes into the Labor Battalions. Any one giving employment to one person for at least one-half year at regular wages earns five points. A single woman who gives up her position in favor of a man in order to be married earns five points.

One point is earned by propaganda—educational work in calling upon ten families. One point can be earned by distributing one hundred placards or propaganda sheets containing the approved speech of a Nazi leader. One or more points can be earned by having repair or building work done to the value of twenty marks. Also, one point can be earned by the purchase of furniture, equipment, clothing and books to the value of twenty marks. One point is earned by installing a radio set, purchasing an automobile, a camera, a bathtub, or a season ticket to the theater, the erection of a home or a gas- and bomb-proof cellar. One point can be earned by voluntary gifts to the National Socialist party of twenty marks or over, by loaning at least one hundred marks to unemployed at low interest rates, by working in National Socialist propaganda in spite of old age or illness. Points can be earned also by marriage and by the birth of any child over and above four children to one marriage. Not only individuals are required to earn these points, but all incorporated companies and organizations. Receipts for purchases which are to be listed in earning points must be furnished upon request by shopkeepers. This ambitious scheme is quite solemnly announced in the press, but it is very much to be doubted if it is ever carried through to full completion.

Promotion of Retail Sales

According to the *Frankfurter Zeitung* of April 5, public employees in Saxony have been reminded that it is their duty to support the German industries and in particular to make all possible purchases of goods for consumption in order to stimulate retail trade. Purchases are to be made particularly in small specialty shops. The department-store chain of Wronker in and around Frankfurt-am-Main was recently closed. According to the *Preussischer Pressedienst,* four hundred and forty-five employees were given new jobs. A certain number of the older employees were able to finance themselves from their savings and the rest were largely Jews who were left to shift by themselves. The inventory was not sold at auction but turned over to smaller shops for sale. According to the *Pressedienst,* there was no disturbance to the economic conditions in Frankfurt by this disappearance of the Wronker stores.

According to the *Berliner Tageblatt* of April 5, the National Socialist party is working on plans with the automobile industry to promote the sale of small passenger cars to employees and officials of German companies. The better paid employees of German industrial firms are to be encouraged to buy passenger cars on long-time payments. In some cases it is suggested that the employing company put up the money and pay themselves back out of the employee's salary. In view of the enthusiasm with which the government is stimulating automobile business it seems quite possible that a good many cars may be sold in this way to people who never really intended to buy them but will have to take their pay partly in automobiles or lose their jobs.

The Minister of Economics has made a public statement to provincial and local governments deprecating the campaign of "buy in your home town." This spirit of local patriotism has gone so far as to encourage purchases in one particular vicinity as against other parts of the town, which is considered by the government to be a disturbing influence in the business situation.

The plan made a few months ago by the German Labor Front for five million go-to-meeting suits for workmen's evening wear has finally been canceled. This action was taken after the Reichsbank had made it quite clear that Germany's exchange situation would not allow the use of additional quantities of wool for this purpose.

Nazi Collectors Get Information from Tax Offices

A conflict has arisen in National Socialist circles in Duesseldorf regarding the right of National Socialist party officials to secure information regarding the financial situation of individuals from the tax authorities. According to a story originally published in the *Deutsche Bergwerks-Zeitung,* the Duesseldorf tax authorities agreed to disclose income-tax and other tax payments of individuals to National Socialist representatives in order that they might investigate the ability of individuals to make voluntary contributions to party funds, and that they might check whether the contributions already made were in fair proportion to the income of the contributors. This decision was taken on the ground that the State and the party have become one, and the State can have no secrets from party representatives. The Duesseldorf action, however, was overruled by the Federal Finance Ministry in a decision of March seventh. This upholds the secrecy of tax payments and forbids tax offices from revealing this confidential information.

Appeals to Foreign Commercial Attachés

A recent court decision in Hamburg is of interest for the work of foreign government representatives in Germany. It was proposed to increase the German import tariff on a certain type of hair used for furniture upholstery. A German spinning company which has been using this material sent a circular letter to other firms and organizations, attempting to prevent the increase in tariff and suggesting that the German firms report the matter to the French commercial representatives and get assistance from the French government in preventing such action. The court of honor of the Hamburg Stock Exchange, which tried the case, decided that this constituted economic treason, and that although it is not punishable under ordinary criminal law, it was a violation of a paragraph of the commercial code. The firm was pronounced guilty but let off with a light punishment since this was a first offense. The case, however, is an interesting one, since according to this decision German firms appealing to the office of the American Commercial Attaché in Berlin for assistance in preventing adverse decisions being taken by the German government are guilty of economic treason and subject to punishment. The case is reported in the *Frankfurter Zeitung* of April twenty-second.

The *Deutsche Bergwerks-Zeitung* of April 11 has reported from Hamburg that German exporting firms who have in former years placed seventy per cent and more of their foreign orders with German manufacturers have now been forced to alter this practice on account of high prices of German goods. According to this statement, in some cases over ninety per cent of such orders coming to Hamburg are placed by the German firms with foreign manufacturers in near-by European countries. When it is considered that there are roughly five thousand of these exporting firms, the amount of business which is being shifted from Germany to other countries in this way must run into very large sums.

20

FOREIGN-EXCHANGE BLOCKADE

Berlin, June 19, 1934

THE FOREIGN-EXCHANGE CRISIS in Germany has reached the point where American firms selling goods in Germany are vitally affected. Since June first, importers are permitted to obtain only ten per cent of the foreign exchange which they were using in the fiscal year 1930-31, or in other words, about five per cent of the quantity of foreign exchange which they were using in more prosperous years. This would already have amounted to a practical embargo on American imports if it were not for several loopholes which have been left open up to now. Unfortunately, these holes have been plugged one after the other.

In the past, it has been possible for importers to take advantage of what are called here *Rembourse* credits—meaning payment by commercial acceptances through American banks under the Standstill Agreement. The extent to which business can be done under commercial acceptances was cut down to twenty per cent of the original quota on June first, and now most importing firms are finding that they are forbidden to use this method of financing their imports. This is particularly true for importers of finished goods.

Imports Through Third Countries Stopped

Similarly, a large amount of American imports have come into Germany in the last few months by taking advantage of the clearing agreements which the German government has made with other European governments. These clearing agreements have now been temporarily suspended as of June eleventh. The Reichsbank states that this was done to prevent third parties from misusing them. There is no doubt that the misuse referred to has principally come about from American firms; for example, one American representative here told me that since his ordinary foreign-exchange quota has been cut away to almost nothing, he has paid for his current imports through the Belgian clearing agreement. In the month of May, he paid in three hundred and fifty thousand marks to the Reichsbank and was reimbursed in Belgian francs through the National Bank of Belgium. Many other American firms have been dealing through Belgium, Holland and other countries. Now apparently the Reichsbank is taking energetic steps to put an end to this practice.

Selling Against Marks

American firms selling goods here are now confronted with the choice of reducing their current business to the amount of foreign exchange which they can actually send out, or of continuing to pile up mark balances which are now untransferable and which may never be paid in dollars. If, on the other hand, such American firms restrict their business to the amount of foreign exchange they could actually remit to the United States, the amount of business is so small that it is not enough to pay for the actual overhead, and they might just as well close up altogether. On the other hand, if they continue to pile up untransferable mark balances, they may be liable to fine or imprisonment under Paragraph 3 of the exchange regulations of April seventeenth. This exchange status was brought to the attention of importers by a circular letter from the Hamburg *Devisenstelle,* dated April 26, 1934. On June ninth, I requested from the Foreign Office a statement as to the exact position of American importers who were currently bringing in more goods than they could pay for, and such a statement has been promised. This may clear the air and enable us to advise importers definitely whether or not they are rendering themselves liable to punishment by this practice.

Sales Against Marks Unwise

Nevertheless, this will be no assistance in deciding the all-important question whether American firms should continue to ship into Germany goods for which they cannot be paid at the present time in dollars. It is my considered opinion that most firms should not do so, that they are probably throwing good money after bad. The balance of probability inclines to the prediction that the present mark must be devaluated. Such devaluation will probably be a drastic one and involve, of course, a heavy loss to foreigners holding mark balances. But this is not the only factor in the situation. I cannot believe that even with such a devaluation the difficulties of trading with Germany will be over. The present National

Socialist experiment is still going on and is leading Germany further away from normal commercial relations with the Western world. Whether eventually this will lead to war, to internal revolution or to the setting up of a wall between Germany and Western countries, is not yet clear, but these things are all possibilities. No one can yet see the way through the morass in which German business and finance are struggling. It is probable that a number of years must elapse before anything like normal commercial relations can be restored. Under these circumstances, American firms that are throwing in new shipments of merchandise against marks are making a very long-shot speculation.

As an example of what is going on, take one American manufacturing company. Their manager tells me that current sales are two hundred thousand marks per month, but that he can transfer to the United States only five thousand marks per month under the present regulations, or one-fortieth of the total. I believe this is taking an undue risk and that the company is in fact practically giving their product away if they continue to ship under these circumstances.

Local Representatives Unwilling to Close Down

Naturally, some local managers of American companies, particularly in manufactured specialties, and German importers, are inclined to keep the existing business going as long as they can; in the first place, it means their own jobs. They are naturally unwilling to discharge their employees and scrap organizations which represent their lifework. Their natural feeling is to hold on a little longer to see whether or not conditions will improve, and to urge their American suppliers to keep on sending enough merchandise to enable the enterprise in Germany to remain alive. This point of view is natural and inevitable, but it is not sound.

Staple Importers Considering Reshipment of Goods

Most of the American firms in Hamburg and Bremen importing staple products from the United States take an entirely different point of view; they are unwilling to sell against marks and thus increase their mark holdings here. They demand dollars or other foreign exchange from German customers. This results in a practical stoppage of business in many lines. The free ports of Germany are full of foreign merchandise which is offered for sale in only foreign exchange. Naturally, it is hoped that foreign exchange may be available later on when the products will be allowed to come into the country. If not, they must be reshipped to other European markets at considerable expense. In the case of some commodities, it is not practicable to reship them elsewhere, since they are suited only for the German market. This is particularly true of sausage casings and to a lesser extent of lard. The only sales of American staple products now going on in German ports against marks are sales of petroleum products by a few of the larger oil companies. A representative of a large United States oil company told me that his firm was selling now against marks, but that they could realize on these marks in several ways, either by constructing oil tankers in Germany, by purchasing steel for pipe lines and casings for oil wells, or by extending their refining and oil drilling operations inside the country.

This shows that there are American enterprises in Germany whose size and peculiar position may give a speculation of this kind more chances of ultimate success; for example, the American oil firms, with refineries and twenty thousand filling stations. The American interests plus the British Shell interests together control the great bulk of the filling stations in Germany and are supplying a commodity which Germany cannot very well produce herself. It seems quite possible that if the British and American oil interests stand together, they may be strong enough to maintain their position and some-day force the Germans to transfer into foreign exchange the mark balances which they are piling up here now. Still, this represents fresh investments in Germany of millions of dollars every year in addition to the enormous stake which they already have in this country.

Difficulty of Transferring Marks

The question naturally arises to what extent American balances here representing current sales of goods can be transferred out of the country at the present time by taking a loss. For the most part this is not possible. The Standstill creditors, namely, foreign banks, have the inside track in getting their funds out of Germany at a discount through the registered mark provision in the Standstill Agreement of 1932. The mark balances built up by current sales of foreign merchandise stand in the name of the German importing firm which may, of course, be entirely owned by an American parent company. Applications to the authorities have frequently been made to allow marks standing in the name of a German subsidiary to be transferred to the American parent company, so that they would become Creditmarks and could be withdrawn from the country under permission of the Reichsbank at a discount. But the foreign-exchange authorities are almost always unwilling to allow such transfers to be made. They explain quite frankly that this would simply result in fresh shipments of foreign goods and another demand for transfer of the proceeds. Furthermore, even if mark balances can be put to the credit of the American exporter in a German bank, the funds still cannot be withdrawn from Germany without special permission from the Reichsbank. These permissions are getting harder to obtain all the time and the discount rate is becoming larger. Even if American owners of blocked funds in Germany are willing to use these marks for the purchase of German goods for sale outside Germany, they are still unable to get permission to take out such goods against their present mark holdings on a basis which will give a profit. At the present time, exporters of German goods are required to turn in the foreign exchange received for their sale to the Reichsbank, and American firms desiring to export German goods against their existing mark balances have been told that they must deposit seventy-five per cent of the foreign-exchange value of the goods with the Reichsbank, giving them the opportunity to reduce their risk in Germany by twenty-five per cent. I understand that recently two American concerns offered to export large additional quantities of German goods on a fifty-per-cent basis, but were refused permission.

Barter Agreements

There finally arises the question of barter arrangements between German and American companies. A great deal has been said on this subject, but almost nothing has been done because of the practical difficulties in the way. I approached the foreign-exchange authorities on this subject about two years ago and was given the answer that they would welcome barter arrangements; that these arrangements should preferably be made between single firms on each side and for staple commodities, if possible, as the more simple arrangements had the better chance of ultimate success; that the application should be made to the foreign-exchange authorities here by the German exporter and that they would in general approve any agreements which could be made on this basis. The German authorities have on several subsequent occasions confirmed the information which they had previously given.

Bartering for Lumber

Last week a new development occurred. One of the largest importers of lumber in Germany visited this office to inform me that he had been selected by the German Ministry of Economics to head a committee of German lumber importers who were instructed to take up with American lumber exporters the question of bartering German finished goods for necessary supplies of American lumber. He stated that the authorities here realize that they need American lumber to the extent of sixty to seventy million marks per year. This comes mainly from the Northwestern and Gulf states. They hope to exchange wire rope, nails, sheets, bars and shapes of iron and steel and other manufactured products, and sell these through importers in the Northwestern and Southern states who would be induced to handle the goods by special price considerations. He stated that the domestic German price for iron and steel products played no part in such a transaction, that these products would simply be exchanged for lumber in such proportions that the sale could be made in America at competitive prices. I pointed out that if prices at which these German goods were imported and sold in the United States were below German prices, this could run counter to the anti-dumping provisions of the American tariff acts.

Difficulties of Negotiation

Several other American export interests are studying the question of bartering their goods for German products, notably American lard exporters and American automobile exporters. Both of these interests have expressed to me their hope that they might exchange these products for German wines and liquors. All of this raises some very far-reaching questions. In the first place, the German goods available for sale in the United States at competitive prices are limited in quantity. There is a tremendous demand here for a wide variety of American products. If barter arrangements are to be effected, who is to decide the question of which American export commodities will be bartered for the few available German goods that come into question? It might prove a great disadvantage to the United States if our cotton, lumber, lard, petroleum, copper and automobile exporters began to compete among themselves for the privilege of handling German wines or other products. Certainly, it is not for American officials in Germany to decide any of these questions or to take any active steps in bringing about such barter arrangements. We have taken the position up to now that these are purely private negotiations. Nevertheless, it would seem that if barter arrangements are actually made, the Departments of State and Commerce and other branches of the American government will have to take an important part in the negotiations and must see to it that any such arrangements are not to the disadvantage of the American public.

On the main question at issue it would seem that the eventual decision is fairly clear and plain, namely, that the American public would be disinclined to purchase heavy additional quantities of German manufactured goods. This would be especially true if the prices quoted were comparable to prices for the same goods in Germany. The American attitude would probably remain the same even if the public were told that such purchases on their part were necessary in order to insure continued sales of American raw materials to Germany. Under these circumstances it would appear that any large-scale attempt to barter German manufactured goods against American raw materials could only achieve very limited success. As regards smaller individual barter arrangements between single German and American firms, there may be some business which can be done in this way, but the practical difficulties are considerable and the possibilities of increasing business are not particularly bright.

Committees Appointed

On inquiry in Hamburg and Bremen, I found that the German Department of Economics has appointed committees for several German trades, not only in the lumber trade but in tobacco, packing-house products, and apparently in other lines. The committees have all been instructed to get in touch with American exporters of such products and arrange to set up, if possible, barter arrangements which will provide additional markets for German goods in the United States against imports of these essential American commodities.

New Controls Expected

German importers point out that Germany now has clearing arrangements with most important foreign countries and expects to make additional arrangements in the future. The system of import controls already set up for many industries will be extended. Both petroleum and tobacco interests inform me that they expect a system to be set up in their trade very soon. It seems logical to expect that under these controls, which will permit imports only against special licenses, the importer will be almost wholly restricted to dealing with countries with which a clearing arrangement already exists. Otherwise he will be refused permission to obtain any foreign exchange. It also seems logical to believe that with the control boards handling almost all the raw materials and food products in whose import Germany is especially interested, little or no foreign exchange will be left for miscellaneous manufactured articles, which will probably remain outside the control system. Such items will probably include automobiles, office equipment, toilet appliances, machine tools and other items of American exports. This will put American goods at a very heavy disadvantage in the German market.

American Trade Hit

Responsible German officials have made no secret of the general plan of the government to reduce imports from the United States more than from other countries. The main reason given for this is the large amount by which American exports to Germany have exceeded imports from Germany in past years. Another very powerful reason is the unwillingness of the government to remain dependent upon overseas sources of supplies for essential commodities. The fear is always present that this trade might be stopped in the event of war. There is no doubt that American sales to Germany will continue to decline during the present year and as long as the present foreign-exchange shortage continues and the present commercial policies of the Government remain in force. There seems little hope of selling certain items of American exports to Germany, for example, manufactured goods and non-essentials. There is, however, likelihood that our sales of staple products will continue. The extent to which we can retain business in Germany differs among commodities.

Cotton

Germany will probably continue to take large quantities of American cotton. Existing stocks are sufficient to run the country for five to six months, but only about one-third of them are paid for; the other two-thirds remain in the hands of Bremen importers and, if foreign exchange cannot be found, could be reshipped elsewhere. The probabilities are that the present stocks in Bremen will all be taken and paid for in dollars and that additional purchases will be made from the new American crop during the fall and winter. The cotton trade believes that the amount of foreign exchange which will be placed at its disposal will be at least fifty per cent of the original foreign-exchange quota. This seems a great deal in comparison with the ten per cent now allowed importers generally. Incidentally, many firms feel that this ten per cent will soon vanish and there will be no foreign exchange whatever granted outside the controlled articles. Under the controls, of course, every permit to import merchandise carries with it the right to secure the necessary amount of foreign exchange.

Tobacco

In the case of tobacco, the situation looks almost hopeless. Present stocks are very low but importers are not disposing of what they have against marks. In most cases they have already sold enough to use up their foreign-exchange quotas for months or even years in advance and will make no further commitments. Unless something can be done for the American tobacco trade in Germany, it will soon be finished. American tobacco, principally Kentucky and Virginia varieties, is used in Germany in smoking mixtures and for chewing tobacco. As soon as a tobacco import control is instituted—and this is expected any day—importers will be largely forced to secure their foreign tobacco from countries with which Germany has a clearing agreement. Such tobacco will replace American tobacco in German brands of smoking and chewing tobacco. The public will gradually learn to consume the new article and lose their taste for the American product, which may never be able to re-enter this market. Incidentally, this happened to American cigarette tobacco which was consumed in Germany before the war. When it was replaced by Near Eastern tobacco, the German public learned to smoke cigarettes of the oriental type; and they never returned to Virginia cigarettes.

Lard

In the case of packing-house products, principally lard, the situation is complicated by a number of unpredictable factors. On paper, the National Socialist self-sufficiency program will virtually exclude American lard and other meat products.

183

In practice, this may prove to be impossible. Our Department of Agriculture representatives here estimate that the domestic German fat supplies plus the quantities of foreign fats allowed to come into Germany under the present regulations will still be about twenty-five per cent below German fat consumption. Furthermore, the present abnormally dry weather has been particularly destructive to the German hay and fodder crops. Farmers are now beginning to slaughter their animals because they are afraid that they cannot feed them over next winter. This should seriously affect the supply of German lard and butter in the coming year and possibly for several years. The fat program may break down and larger import contingents from abroad become necessary, always provided Germany can secure the foreign exchange to pay for them.

As against these facts, there can be cited the opinion of one of the shrewdest packing representatives in Hamburg who admits that lard, butter and margarine supplies will be below consumption needs, but says that Germany still has an excess of fat pork and that the poorer classes of the population will be forced to give up butter, lard and margarine and eat fat pork or render it out at home, a course of action which would not affect their health but would simply be a reduction in the existing standard of living.

Earning Overhead

The American firms engaged in distribution of packing-house products in Germany are not able to meet operating expenses out of their current sales of American goods, owing to their low foreign-exchange quotas, already mentioned. They are, however, managing to keep alive by doing all sorts of other business, for example, selling to countries outside Germany, importing goods from other European countries with which Germany has clearing agreements, and selling and buying German meat products. In this way they can keep on going, but this does not mean anything in the way of increasing American exports. This same state of affairs obtains in other trades.

Dollar and Mark Price Spread

It is interesting to note that a definite scale of prices for the same product has been set up, depending on the character of the means of payment. For example, a given quantity of lard in Hamburg is sold at a reasonably low price in dollars, if the customer has dollars to pay for it. If the customer merely has a permit to pay through some clearing agreement with a foreign country, the price is higher because the importer who pays in marks at the Reichsbank cannot know for several weeks the rate of exchange at which the exporter will be reimbursed in the foreign country. There is a margin of risk here, and also a risk that a permit may be canceled or the clearing agreement break down in the meantime. This causes the difference in price. A third and still higher price is quoted for the same product if the German customer can only pay in untransferable marks. American firms are not interested in this business at any price, but some other firms, especially the Dutch, have been taking business of this kind, attracted by the higher prices. It is thus interesting to see that already the free mark is devalued as against foreign currencies in Germany, quite aside from the much lower value of the registered mark, the *Kredit-Rueckzahlungs-Mark* and the *Effekten-Mark,* the last two of which are about fifty per cent of the value of the free mark.

Mark Devaluation Expected

This spread, between the internal value of the mark and its theoretical gold par, clearly shows the increasing difficulties which the Reichsbank is facing in holding the mark at its present parity. About half of the German businessmen whom I have recently interviewed believe that the mark will be devaluated in the course of the present financial crisis, probably somewhat later in the year. The other half still believe that the political disadvantages of tampering with currency will restrain the government from any action of this kind. It is my personal belief that devaluation must and will take place, but only after the government has tried out several other measures in an attempt to improve Germany's balance of payments. The first important move in this respect will probably be the creation of a general government import monopoly, supervising all the existing control boards for specific raw materials and foodstuffs. The German press carried last night an official statement that a new consolidation of import controls was imminent and that in view of this forthcoming step no changes should be made in existing foreign-trade organizations until further notice.

Possible Export Bounty System

The second government move which can be expected is some sort of premium or bounty scheme on German exports. This will replace to a great extent the existing method of subsidies through the use of scrip, which has proved cumbersome and unsatisfactory. The chief complaint which German exporters have uttered regarding the use of scrip for export subsidies is the fact that an exporter cannot know in advance how much scrip he will be allotted on an individual transaction nor what the rate of discount on his complete transaction will be. Thus, the German exporter cannot quote fixed prices in foreign markets and is uncertain whether he can afford to underbid competing firms from other countries or not. If he attempts to make a tentative contract with a foreign buyer and to hold the business open until he can receive definite word from the Gold Discount Bank what his total discount on the transaction will be, the customer is likely to buy from other quarters in the meantime.

Easing of Foreign-exchange Crisis Expected

Any form of export bounties which may be worked out will probably run foul of existing anti-dumping legislation in foreign countries or may evoke new retaliatory legislation of this type. It does not seem likely that Germany's export trade can be substantially benefited by such means. Nevertheless, the government is bound to make the attempt before taking the last dreaded step of currency devaluation. In the meantime, existing German foreign trade will continue to fall. It seems likely that the present drastic restrictions on imports will probably bring them below exports by midsummer and thus secure a small active trade balance. It is expected here by the most competent observers that the Reichsbank position will be somewhat improved in the late summer and the foreign-exchange situation will become a little easier after the full effect of the present import restrictions is felt. The general effect of this situation will be a reduction in the German standard of living, which will probably continue for an indefinite period. How long the German public will cheerfully accept privations of this kind without attempting to fix the blame upon the present government, is still an open question. Thoughtful Germans, of course, realize that their country's present commercial and financial difficulties are only partly the result of the National Socialist economic setup, and are largely attributable to outside circumstances which no one in this country can control.

21

NEW SYSTEM OF IMPORT CONTROL

Berlin, September 19, 1934

IN HIS RECENT ADDRESSES at the Leipzig Fall Fair and at the International Farm Conference at Eilsen, Dr. Schacht outlined the main features of his new plan for regulating German foreign trade. They can be briefly summarized as follows:

1. Strict adjustment of imports to Germany's ability to pay and to her available reserves of foreign exchange. This implies an extension of the already existing control of certain raw materials to practically all imported goods. It also means the abandonment of the old system of general foreign-exchange permits issued to individual firms and of the day-to-day allocation of foreign exchange by the Reichsbank, which in practice had created an impossible situation, as demonstrated by the increasing inability of importers to pay for goods already delivered.

2. Revision of the present system of bilateral clearing agreements, which on the one hand are leading to a shrinking of foreign trade, and on the other hand are piling up untrans-

ferable mark balances in the accounts of the Reichsbank, opened in the name of foreign central banks.

3. Development of domestic sources of raw materials, with a view to replacing the imported product. This aim, Dr. Schacht stressed, is to be achieved by all available means, even regardless of the higher cost of domestic substitutes.

4. Promotion of exports with increased energy by utilizing all possibilities of scrip and bond repurchases, and simultaneous rejection of both devaluation and deflation as means of stopping the shrinkage of German export trade.

Scope and Effect of New Control Measures

To carry into effect the first objective of the "New Plan," namely, the adjustment of current imports to available means of payments, is the purpose of a whole system of measures embodied in the following administrative acts:

1. A decree relative to Trade in Commodities of September 4, 1934 (*Verordnung ueber den Warenverkehr vom 4. September 1934, Reichsgesetzblatt, Teil 1, No. 102*).

2. A decree of September 4, 1934, regarding the establishment of import control boards (*Verordnung ueber die Errichtung von Ueberwachungsstellen, Deutscher Reichsanzeiger* of September 7, 1934).

3. An administrative order (No. I/34) of the Federal Foreign Exchange Board to all import control boards, regarding the principles to be adopted for the issuance of the new foreign-exchange certificates (published in the German daily press on September 3, 1934).

4. A decree of September 11, 1934, amending certain provisions of the foreign-exchange regulations now in force (*Verordnung zur Aenderung der Verordnung ueber die De-*

visenbewirtschaftung vom 11. September 1934, Deutscher Reichsanzeiger of September 11, 1934).

The new regulations are bound to restrict materially the freedom of action of the individual importer. While under the old system he was assigned a monthly quota, however small, within which he was at liberty to buy any goods that fell within his regular line of business, the main objective of the new regulations is to subject every individual import transaction to an elaborate licensing procedure. This will permit a greater degree of discrimination between essential and non-essential imports already introduced in regard to raw materials by the Act of March 22, 1934, and henceforth to be applied to virtually all imports. Official pronouncements leave little doubt that under this system of discrimination there will hardly be any foreign exchange available for the importation of manufactured goods; only a small quantity of these will probably be imported under the various clearing agreements while all available foreign exchange will be applied to the purchase of raw materials and such foodstuffs as Germany must still import.

Organization of New Control Boards

The decree relative to Trade in Commodities of September fourth, 1934, partly extends and partly replaces the so-called *Rohstoffgesetz* or Raw Materials Act of March 22, 1934. The system of import control boards (*Ueberwachungsstellen*), heretofore limited to the main groups of imported raw materials, is to be applied in the future to all goods imported into Germany, whether raw materials, semi-manufactures or finished products. The decree authorizes the Minister of Economics, in conjunction, when necessary, with the Minister of Food and Agriculture, not only to supervise and regulate the importation of these goods, but also to issue regulations relative to the latter's distribution, warehousing, sale and consumption. To this purpose he can organize control boards (*Ueberwachungsstellen*), which possess the status rights of a juristic person. The Minister of Economics also appoints Federal Commissioners (*Reichsbeauftragte*) who are put in charge of the individual control boards and are directing their activities in accordance with orders and instructions received from the Minister of Economics. A special advisory council can be attached to each commissioner. Its members are designated by the Minister of Economics. The expenses of the control boards are to be covered by special fees and assessments. The Minister of Economics is to issue regulations relative to the collection of these fees from persons and firms subject to the jurisdiction of the individual control board. The violation of regulations issued by the control boards is to be punished either by imprisonment or imposition of a fine; and no maximum limit is set for this latter.

The twenty-five control boards established under the new régime consist of the three following groups.

I. Eleven control boards already established under the Raw Materials Act of March 22, 1934, for the following products:

1. Tobacco
2. Industrial Fats
3. Wool and Other Animal Hair
4. Cotton
5. Cotton Yarn
6. Bast Fibers
7. Hides and Skins
8. Rubber and Asbestos
9. Carbon Black
10. Non-Precious Metals
11. Iron and Steel

II. Four control boards for agricultural products; it has been agreed between the Minister of Economics and the Minister of Food and Agriculture that the following monopoly boards for agricultural products will act as import control boards for the various goods subject to their jurisdiction, under instructions issued by the Minister of Economics:

1. Monopoly Board for Grain, Fodder and Other Agricultural Products
2. Monopoly Board for Animals and Animal Products
3. Monopoly Board for Milk Products, Oils and Fats
4. Monopoly Board for Eggs

III. Ten new control boards regulating imports of all commodities not covered by any of the organizations indicated in the preceding two groups for the following products:

1. Wood
2. Vegetables, Fruit, Beverages, and Other Foodstuffs
3. Coal and Salt
4. Mineral Oils
5. Chemicals
6. Silk, Rayon, Clothing, and Similar Products
7. Furs
8. Paper
9. Technical Products
10. Miscellaneous Products

There has been published in the *Deutsche Reichsanzeiger* of September 18 (No. 218), a complete list of all imported commodities based on the classification of the German Customs Tariff and indicating to which of the twenty-five import control boards each of these commodities has been allocated.

Out of the twenty-five control boards, twenty-two are located in Berlin, two in Bremen (cotton and tobacco) and one in Leipzig (furs).

The "Foreign-exchange Certificate"

The old system of general foreign-exchange permits had to be abandoned for two reasons: first, it did not allow a sufficient discrimination between goods considered of vital importance and other merchandise; second, from the moment that, at the end of June, the Reichsbank had to resort to a day-to-day allocation of foreign exchange, importers had no guaranty whatsoever that they would actually obtain the amount of foreign exchange to which they were theoretically entitled under their permits.

In the future, a foreign-exchange certificate (*Devisenbescheinigung*) must be applied for and issued for every individual import transaction. Importation of goods for which no such certificate has been issued is not prohibited; but the importer cannot expect to obtain the permission to pay for them when the payment becomes due.

"Cash" and "Credit" Certificates

The foreign-exchange certificate is required for all payments relative to import transactions as defined by the decree on foreign-exchange control of May 23, 1932, and its subsequent amendments. Thus, the new certificates issued by the Import Control Boards will replace the former foreign-exchange permits, either general or issued for individual transactions by the Foreign Exchange Offices (*Devisenstellen*).

There will, however, be two different kinds of certificates. The one already described in the preceding paragraph will authorize the firm to which it has been issued to make payments for imported goods within a specified short period, and will also serve as a kind of official guaranty that the importer

will actually obtain the amount required from the Reichsbank. This will apply to goods bought on a cash basis, for
prompt shipment, or from stocks lying in one of the free ports
or bonded warehouses. However, apart from these "cash certificates" the Import Control Boards will have the power to
issue a "binding assurance" (*Verbindliche Zusage*) that the
importer will obtain the required amount of foreign exchange when the goods arrive (if bought for forward shipment), or when the draft becomes due (if bought on several
months' credit).

Official instructions already issued in this connection leave
no doubt that the issue of certificates for cash payment will be
restricted as far as possible, since the amounts of foreign exchange available for this purpose are exceedingly limited. The
control boards are further instructed to see that all possibilities for imports on a credit basis are fully utilized. Certificates
for cash payment are to be refused when credit purchases in
the respective trade are customary. If the total amount of
foreign exchange applied for by different importers of a given
commodity exceeds the amount made available for this purpose by the Reichsbank, preference is to be given to those firms
whose foreign suppliers are offering the best credit terms.

While the main object of this reform is to establish an equi-
librium between Germany's imports and her foreign-exchange
reserves, and thus to reassure the individual importer that he
will obtain the foreign exchange required when he actually
needs it, this discrimination between two kinds of certificates
(for cash payments and for credits) obviously brings a certain
element of uncertainty into the whole scheme. The import
control boards and the Reichsbank will have to give "binding assurances," in regard to payments which will become due
six, nine, or even more months ahead. Since, under present
circumstances, it is exceedingly difficult to foresee the move-

ment of German exports and the amount of foreign exchange they will yield even a few months from now, the controlling authorities will have to follow a very conservative policy in issuing these "binding assurances" for future credits.

Filing of Applications

Applications for foreign-exchange certificates have to be filed with the Import Control Board which is competent for the respective commodity. If for the execution of one order a firm requires different imported materials which fall within the jurisdiction of several control boards, the company may file one application for all these materials with the control board which is competent for the finished product. In this case, the firm must produce an affidavit to the effect that no duplicating applications for the same materials have been filed with other control boards. The control board which receives such a "combined" application passes the applications for individual materials to the respective boards for action and decision, and, ultimately, distributes to the applicant the individual certificates issued by all control boards concerned. The purpose of this somewhat complicated procedure is to prevent a firm from obtaining certificates from one board for some of the materials required, while, in regard to other materials to be used for the same order, its application is rejected by other control boards.

Issue of Certificates to Importers

One of the basic principles of the new procedure is that a foreign-exchange certificate will be issued only when the ultimate manufacturer or consumer of the imported material is designated. This is considered necessary, because only in this way is it possible to determine whether the material in question is indispensable, and also whether the same application has not been "duplicated" by having been filed simultaneously both by the manufacturer (consumer) and the prospective importer. However, the government emphatically denies any intention on its part to encourage the manufacturer to make his purchases direct from the foreign supplier.

On the contrary, the certificate will, as a matter of principle, be issued only in the name of an importer, but on condition that the ultimate manufacturer, in order to avoid speculative trading in foreign exchange certificates, indicate the importer through whom he intends to import, and in whose name the certificate will be made out. Exceptions from this general rule can only be granted and certificates issued in the name of a manufacturer in cases where the latter can prove that he has always been purchasing the goods direct from exporters in a foreign country and has made direct payment for them. Likewise, by way of exception, certificates can be issued to importers without designating the name of the manufacturer in regard to such commodities, as the import trade has, as a rule, been buying at its own risk and for its own account.

22

CONTROL OFFICES AND OUR
TRADE WITH GERMANY

Berlin, September 26, 1934

THE NEW FOREIGN-EXCHANGE restrictions, which went into effect on September 24 in Germany, provide an entirely new situation for the American exporter. These regulations set up twenty-five import control offices covering all commodities. In the future, payment in foreign exchange will only be made in cases where the German importer has in advance procured a permit from the German government, covering the specific transaction in which the price paid for the goods and their destination are stated.

From now on, American firms can no longer expect to be paid for goods shipped on consignment or for goods shipped on open account to their German customers. From now on, it seems unlikely that American firms will be able to maintain a profitable business through a German agent unless they are shipping some commodity which is in special demand. It is no longer worth while for our companies to cultivate the

German market, to advertise or to solicit business by letter or personal visit, except in very special cases, nor can they approach the German government in the hope of securing an order.

All requests for permits to pay for foreign merchandise must be made by the German users of such merchandise. In most cases this will be a manufacturer who uses foreign raw materials. In some cases, however, where the importing trade has been accustomed to import on its own account and sell later to manufacturers, this method may be adhered to. From now on, German firms which have been granted a permit will then contact foreign suppliers, principally of raw materials, and place their orders. It may be assumed that such orders will be filled largely from stocks lying in the free ports of Hamburg and Bremen. It will probably pay a certain number of American firms to maintain such stocks in these free ports in the hope that German orders will materialize and with the assurance that the goods may be sold outside Germany without interference from the German government. This assurance has been given repeatedly.

Cash and Credit Permits

Our sales to Germany can be divided into two classes, (1) those in which the permit allows immediate payment in cash, and (2) those in which the payment is financed through the use of ordinary acceptance credits, utilizing the funds held in Germany by foreign banks under the Standstill Agreement. The German government proposes to restrict permits calling for immediate payment in cash to a minimum and is attempting to secure longer credit terms than has been customary up to now for most raw-material items. A three-page secret instruction has been issued by the Reichsbank regarding the allocation of Standstill funds for acceptance credits, but great care has been taken that the wording of these regulations does not become known in creditor countries. It is believed that they embody a reduction in the total amount of purchases and a reallocation among commodities in order to provide Germany with certain essential products of which a scarcity exists.

Barter Agreements

There remains another method of selling to Germany, namely, through the application of barter agreements. These agreements require no official sanction in the United States but do require sanction by the German government. In most cases they are purely private agreements between German and American exporters and provide that payments against certain American goods sold in Germany shall be placed in a special account with the Reichsbank from which specified German goods sold in the United States will be paid. The new regulations for barter agreements specify that in the case of certain essential imports, barter will be allowed on a one-to-one basis, i.e., one hundred dollars' worth of American goods may be imported against taking of one hundred dollars' worth of certain German goods in the United States. However, when the barter agreement applies to imports which are not considered of primary necessity, it is provided that the foreign exporter must agree to take an amount of German goods larger in value than the amount which he imports. A usual margin of thirty per cent is provided for in the published regulations, but the authorities are in some cases more severe. For example, the recent agreement made by the California

Walnut Growers' Association provided that they must purchase twice as much in value from Germany as their sales here.

Germans Unwilling to Barter on Even Basis

This raises the question as to whether all American firms making such barter agreements ought not to get together to prevent the imposition of such handicaps. On the other hand it would appear to me that the German government is over-reaching itself by making such stipulations, and the result will be either that the foreign exporter is unable to dispose of German goods in sufficient quantity, so that the deal will fall to the ground, or that a comparatively small amount of American goods will be tied up in barter agreements for a larger amount of German exports to the United States, so that when it is found that German exports to America cannot be expanded much above these figures, other essential imports from America will be brought in and paid for in cash.

Decree Against Price Increases

This is not the only point at which the German government is hampering trade by over-severe regulations. As reported by cable yesterday, a decree has just been made public forbidding the sale in Germany of a certain number of foreign products, which are to be specified later, at prices unreasonably higher than corresponding prices outside Germany. It is provided that a certain increase based upon shipping costs and a reasonable profit will be permitted. This regulation is designed to counteract the growing tendency of firms handling foreign products to ask higher prices inside

Germany on the basis of existing scarcity. It seems unlikely that this tendency can be successfully combated merely by the issuance of a government regulation. As such goods become increasingly scarce and desirable, they will, in the very nature of things, command a higher price, which must be paid either in cash or in some other form, or perhaps by diluting or altering the quality of the goods. It seems quite logical that American companies, carrying stocks of materials in the free ports, must be duly recompensed for the additional risks and expenses under the existing regulations and, in particular, must be paid for their service in maintaining stocks here without knowing whether or not they may eventually be able to dispose of them. As a matter of fact, prices quoted inside Germany on staple commodities are now higher than world prices, even allowing for the difference due to import tariffs, freight charges, etc., and no decree of a German government can succeed in holding prices down.

American Chamber of Commerce Barter Committee

Within the last few days, the number of inquiries made at this office in regard to barter arrangements has been increasing. I do not see how an American government representative in Germany can take an active part in bringing American and German firms together in negotiations of this kind, nor do I believe that it is proper for us to approach the German government with a request that specific barter arrangements be made. I have, therefore, with the approval of the Embassy, asked the American Chamber of Commerce in Berlin to set up a committee which would undertake to assist American exporters in barter agreements, promising that this office, of course, will do everything it can in the way of advising and helping American firms, but stating that we cannot take an active part in such arrangements. The Chamber has willingly undertaken this task.

Expert Testimony on Spare Parts

I have also asked the Chamber of Commerce committee to take steps to inaugurate another service which should prove very useful to American exporters in this market, namely, the securing of qualified experts who can give testimony under oath before the German government offices regarding the character of the proposed imports. To illustrate the nature of this service, take the case of spare parts for automobiles, office equipment and miscellaneous machinery. There are now operating in Germany many thousands of American automobiles, a great number of American adding and calculating machines, typewriters, vacuum cleaners, electric refrigerators, not to speak of machine tools, printing machinery and many other mechanical devices. It seems unlikely that foreign-exchange permits can be secured for the importation of complete new machines, but the existing machines must be serviced with replacement parts as they wear out, or else the German owners will suffer severe losses and inconvenience.

The German Ministry of Economics realizes this fact and has told me that imports of spare parts will be permitted and foreign-exchange permits will be furnished on the basis of applications, made by German firms, supported by the testimony of qualified German experts under oath, that the spare parts in question are at present neither manufactured in Germany nor can be easily manufactured in Germany and that they are necessary for the operation of existing equipment. The Ministry of Economics is particularly anxious to prevent the import of large quantities of foreign spare parts which might later be assembled to form new complete machines in evasion of the government's intention.

Qualified experts under oath are available in Germany through the courts and more particularly through the semi-official Chambers of Commerce. The American Chamber of Commerce in Berlin through its close connection with the semi-official *Industrie-und Handelskammer* will be able to secure the services of these experts and put them at the service of interested American firms. The fees for such services will, of course, be passed on to the German consumer. Such qualified experts will also prove useful in presenting testimony that certain desired imports are actual essentials and should be bartered for, on a one-to-one basis.

There will apparently be a great demand for services of this kind in future months. A number of private agencies in Germany, including some of the newspapers, such as the *Frankfurter Zeitung* and the *Berliner Tageblatt,* are inaugurating special departments to take care of applications for barter business. I was told last week that barter applications had been coming to the foreign-exchange offices in Hamburg so fast that they were no longer able to handle them and have turned the whole lot over to the Hamburg Chamber of Commerce to study.

Unsatisfactory Nature of Barter System

It seems likely that the number of barter agreements which are actually concluded and which result in satisfactory business may not be more than one to a hundred of the applications. I do not believe that these barter deals are going to work out very satisfactorily or result in very much new business. Nevertheless, when an American exporter desires to attempt an arrangement of this kind, he merits our assistance and support as far as we are at liberty to help him.

Unwillingness to Export on Barter

An unexpected difficulty has arisen in arranging barter transactions, namely, that the new control offices are showing an unwillingness to allow certain German goods to be exported in barter for necessary imports. Whether this arises from fear of domestic shortage for military or other purposes, or whether it is simply the reluctance of newly appointed officials to commit themselves without being fully posted on all details of the new national policy, is not clear. The fact is that at this moment the control offices are unwilling to allow most German products to be specified as exports to the United States under barter arrangements. They are probably awaiting more complete instructions, but do not know from whom. The Ministry of Economics and the Reichsbank are equally in the dark on this point. Everybody is afraid of running counter to orthodox National Socialist policy, but nobody knows what National Socialist policy is, probably not even Hitler.

Another disputed point: which German exports are to be considered as additional exports? Practical businessmen here are taking the point of view that, at present, German sales to the United States are so low and prospects for improvement are so unpromising that practically all German goods exported to the United States of America ought to be considered additional exports and so become eligible as legitimate objects of barter. In this question, as in others, time and the resulting pressure of demand here for foreign materials will undoubtedly bring the solution and will cause the control offices to be less exacting in their stipulations. For the moment, the new officials are so confused and uncertain that it is practically impossible to get their consent to any sort of a transaction, no matter how desirable it may seem.

It is still too early to make any general statement as to how the new regulations will work out. Most of the control boards have already been set up and are now functioning in an ineffective way. It will take some weeks before they really are able to make up their own minds how much of each commodity they are going to allow in, and what kind of credit terms they can successfully insist upon, and what German products will be offered in exchange. This, of course, involves a tug-of-war with foreign suppliers, such as is now going on with the British cotton trade. The general effect must, of course, be to reduce German imports further. If the control offices are successful they may succeed in diverting some of the existing American trade to other countries whose takings of German goods are more satisfactory from their point of view. Nevertheless, the trade balance with the United States still remains very heavily in America's favor and is likely to continue so in spite of all regulations, as the Germans desperately need many of the products we have to sell and prices on their products are so high as to make sales in the United States difficult—quite irrespective of any attitude on the part of the American public for or against German goods.

23

RAW-MATERIAL OUTLOOK

Berlin, October 11, 1934

THE GERMAN RAW-MATERIAL situation during the next six months will primarily be determined by:

1. Available stocks and the rate at which they are being consumed by industry, and
2. Current imports.

Little or no immediate relief can be expected from the development of domestic substitutes, in spite of the active propaganda that is being carried on in this respect. An increase in the production of rayon and other artificial fibers may improve, to a certain extent, the situation in textile industries within a year or so, but the realization of far-reaching plans, now contemplated, for a substantial increase in domestic (synthetic) gasoline output will require several years. The various suggestions for saving or stretching available supplies of raw materials, part of which are already being enforced by law (e.g., the prohibitions of the use of non-ferrous metals) may have a more immediate effect upon consumption of imported materials, although their adverse influence upon both cost and quality of the finished products seems unavoidable.

While import figures permit certain conclusions regarding the probable state of supplies in all industries, statistical data relative to current consumption and stocks are only available in certain cases. Nevertheless, the material briefly summarized below does not indicate that any spectacular breakdown of German industrial production owing to shortage of foreign raw materials can be anticipated for the next two or three months, i.e., before the end of 1934. Stocks from abnormally high imports during the first half of the year, economy measures, and current though curtailed imports, will enable industry to carry on at reduced schedules. As regards imports, they were, in spite of all restrictive measures, maintained remarkably well till the end of August (wool being one of the most important exceptions). How the position will develop in the new year, will therefore chiefly depend on the volume of imports during the remaining months of 1934.

Textile Materials

At the end of June, 1934, the *Institut fuer Konjunkturforschung* published an estimate according to which stocks of textile materials available in Germany corresponded approximately to four to five months' industrial consumption. A more recent estimate (the *Institut's* quarterly report released early in October) asserts that during the past three months these stocks have been reduced by about one-third. This would mean that stocks still available at the end of the third quarter would last for about three months, even if current imports were altogether stopped.

Cotton

From January to May, 1934, imports of raw cotton and linters were materially higher than in 1933. During the first eight months of 1934 cotton imports were eighteen per cent higher than in the corresponding period of last year (273,650 tons against 236,400 tons). No statistical data of industrial stocks are available. During the first eight months of the year (until the decree restricting work in textile mills to thirty-six hours per week became effective) most cotton mills were operating to capacity, many of them worked overtime. In June, the production index in the cotton industry was 118.7 as against 99.9 in 1933 (monthly average) and 100 in the "prosperity" year 1928. Thus, the greater part of excess imports during the first half of the year was probably consumed, as indicated by the above-mentioned estimate of the *Institut fuer Konjunkturforschung,* relating to all textile materials. Yet industry, whose current consumption of cotton, owing to restricted output and gradually increasing use of substitutes, has been reduced by some twenty-five per cent (compared with the first half-year), can still rely upon current imports which in August, 1934 (24,383 tons) were only twenty-seven per cent below the 1933 monthly average.

Wool

The position in the wool industry is less satisfactory. Both stocks and current imports have declined more heavily than in the case of cotton. Industrial stocks of washed wool (which, of course, are only part of the total) were relatively well maintained throughout the first eight months of the year. However, in August, 1934, they were ninety per cent below the 1933 figure. Stocks of combed wool declined from their peak figure of 8,155 tons in March last to 5,146 tons in August. The latter figure was forty-six per cent below the corresponding figure for the same month of 1933. Imports of raw wool showed a rise in the first half of 1934, when they amounted to 139,070 tons against 116,153 tons in 1933—an increase of twenty per cent. However, owing to more stringent restrictions of new purchases abroad than in the case of cotton, imports fell rather abruptly from the peak figure of 26,937 tons in April, 1934 to 3,917 tons in August, the latter figure representing only twenty-seven per cent of monthly average wool imports in 1933. An adjustment of restricted production to current imports appears more difficult than in regard to cotton; but, according to credible trade opinion, no catastrophic situation is likely to arise before the end of 1934.

Hides and Skins

The German leather industry is dependent on imported raw hides and skins for more than fifty per cent of its consumption. As in most other industries, tanners' stocks were substantially raised by the large imports of the first six months of 1934. In its last quarterly report, the *Institut fuer Konjunkturforschung* estimates stocks of raw hides at forty-nine million marks at the end of June, 1934. These stocks, the *Institut* asserts, would alone suffice to cover the needs of industry for a period of four months. In July, consumption exceeded for the first time current supplies of hides, domestic and foreign, so that stocks registered a small decline, as demonstrated by the "Hide Balance" of the German leather industry as computed by the *Institut*. This decline will no doubt proceed at an accelerated rate during the remainder of the year, yet available stocks will probably suffice to cover the deficit till well into the new year.

Iron and Steel

The German pig iron industry is largely dependent on imported ore. In 1933 over eighty-five per cent of ore consumed (due allowance being made for the iron contents of the poorer domestic ores) was imported from foreign countries, notably France, Sweden and Spain. In spite of all efforts to develop domestic deposits, this ratio is not likely to be materially altered during the next few years, as far as pig iron is concerned, though better utilization of scrap may help to raise the steel output without corresponding increase of the imported raw material.

Stocks of imported iron ore at the steel mills are considerable. The *Institut fuer Konjunkturforschung* estimated at the beginning of July that if the 1934 pig iron output should reach the 1930 level, it will suffice to cover nine months' consumption. Besides, imports of iron ore during the summer months were maintained at a high level, proportionate to the increase of pig iron production since the beginning of the year. Thus in August, 1934, imports of iron ore amounted to 868,651 tons compared with 477,057 tons during the same month of 1933.

Imports of manganese ore were also considerably higher than last year. In August they amounted to 18,629 tons against 8,373 tons during the corresponding month of 1933. Even if part of the stocks on hand at the end of June should be consumed by now, the balance will probably suffice to carry the industry through the winter months without necessitating a material reduction of operation schedules.

Non-Ferrous Metals

Imports of all non-ferrous metals were abnormally high during the first half of 1934 and, in spite of increased consumption, must have helped to build up substantial stocks. Restrictive measures caused a serious drop of imports only from July, 1934. Still, in August, 1934, copper imports were only sixteen per cent below the 1933 monthly average. Meanwhile, current consumption of imported non-ferrous metals has, according to trustworthy trade opinion, been reduced at least by fifteen per cent, owing to the substitution of domestically produced aluminum and to other economy measures. Therefore, unless imports are materially reduced in the coming months below their August level, the position of industries consuming large quantities of non-ferrous metals, especially that of the electrical industry, is not likely to become critical before the end of the new year.

24

FACING THE FACTS

Berlin, October 25, 1934

ON SEPTEMBER 24, 1934, a new system for the control of Germany's import trade came into effect. Under this system, twenty-five import control offices pass upon the desirability of the purchase of all foreign goods. Permission to pay in foreign exchange is granted to an importer only on the basis of a specific permit for each transaction. So severe is the present foreign-exchange shortage and so disorganized are the government departments in the initial weeks of the new system that very few import permits carrying the right for payment in foreign exchange have, in fact, been granted since the new system went into effect a month ago.

This brings American exporters to Germany and American firms carrying on business in Germany face to face with a new situation. They must either drastically restrict their existing business, perhaps pulling out altogether, or they must continue to sell against marks and pile up assets inside Germany. Many of these firms are still continuing business in their old manner through force of habit or because their local representatives are unwilling to terminate existing arrangements which, incidentally, provide them with a livelihood. Some of these representatives are saying that for the present it may be worth while to build up untransferable mark-balances inside Germany. They hope the situation will improve in a short time—and then American firms can get their money. But Schacht has publicly stated that any goods brought into Germany for which foreign exchange permits are not secured will not be paid for in foreign exchange in the foreseeable future. This is no time for American companies to drift along, vaguely hoping that some improvement is going to take place. It is necessary to face the facts of the German situation; some of these can be briefly set forth as follows.

No Peaceful Evolution Possible in Germany

I. The existing National Socialist government in Germany is essentially a government of force. In spite of the fact that it achieved power through apparently legal means, it does not rest upon legal methods and is not dependent upon popular support today. It is a pure dictatorship. The leading figures in the National Socialist movement, such as Hitler, Goering, Goebbels, and the rest, have burned their bridges behind them. They cannot surrender power and return peaceably to private life. Their only course is to retain power by all methods or to be thrown out by violence, probably to meet a violent death. There is no country in the world where these men could be safe if they lost power in Germany. Since this government is essentially a dictatorship maintained by force, it cannot evolve peaceably into another form of government. History proves fairly conclusively that a dictatorship based on force usually comes to a violent end sooner or later. This means that the existing National Socialist government will go on, subject to minor changes, of course, but without losing its identity until it is brought to an end either by foreign war, internal revolution, or both.

National Socialist Government Will Last Several Years

II. There is no change now in sight in Germany. The existing government has complete control of the army, the police, and the large party armies of the S.S., *Arbeitsdienst*, Hitler Youth, etc. The government has complete control of the press, the radio, public meetings, transportation, public utilities. It controls the stocks of essential commodities and has both the will and the means to maintain itself in power even against very strong dissatisfaction on the part of the public. At the present time, only part of the public is dissatisfied. This comprises mainly the better-educated groups. Although a certain amount of disillusionment has spread through the masses, many of them are still hopeful that National Socialist Germany will give them a livable future, and very few persons in Germany are capable at the present time of making an open stand against the government. The experience of other countries shows how successfully a strong dictatorial government may continue in power even if numbers of the population are in concealed opposition. Indeed, it seems likely that at the present time Hitler can count upon stronger popular support than Mussolini. We should be most skeptical regarding rumors and alarming stories emanating from Berlin or outside Germany that the National Socialist régime is cracking and that a speedy change is in sight. Such rumors accompanied the early years of the Fascist experiment and will probably continue to arise regarding the Hitler government, but they must all be very heavily discounted. A sober unprejudiced examination of the present situation in Germany indicates that the National Socialist movement will go on and the party remain in control for at least some years.

Economic Situation Bound to Grow Worse

III. We may expect the general situation in Germany to grow slowly but steadily worse under National Socialist administration. In the immediate future, we may expect a continuance of the domestic boom caused by the government's policy of construction and military expenditures, financed by government short-term borrowing. This movement is slowly raising the cost of living and raising prices of agricultural and manufactured articles. Through the various employment measures and the restriction in the free movement of labor, actual shortages of labor in certain trades have arisen in parts of the country; for example, in Berlin it is getting more difficult to find domestic help; it is quite difficult to hire a competent mechanic, while plasterers, paper hangers and other skilled workmen in the building trade have for some months been fully employed. Some four millions of people have been re-employed in the last year and a half, although mostly at very low wages and partly through a policy of sharing work.

Many party functionaries or party members have done well financially; for example, a check-up on one fashionable street in the West End of Berlin showed that twenty-four large villas have been offered for sale there in the past year; twenty of them have already found purchasers, generally from among those who have been enriched by the new régime. Many persons in Germany are spending money, some of them more freely than was their habit a year or two ago; popular psychology has been to some extent changed; people are expecting higher prices and fearing eventual currency depreciation; there is now a tendency to withdraw money from the banks and to spend it for commodities. For example, soap has been hoarded so rapidly in the last few weeks that it is hard to purchase it now. The manager of a large group of chain stores stated last week that many of his branches were completely out of soap and could not get more supplies at present. This flight into commodities and away from the mark stimulates all sorts of business and enlivens the general scene. It is getting difficult to buy a ticket at a Berlin motion picture theater or find a seat in a café in the evening, although the average customer spends only small amounts.

Raw Material Shortage in Spring of 1935

But this apparent movement is an unhealthy and artificial one, partly based upon credit inflation and partly upon fear. Stocks of foreign raw materials are shrinking. A careful examination of the existing stocks, the rate of consumption and the possible imports in the next few months leads to the conclusion, which has been checked in a number of different quarters, that the shortage of foreign raw materials will become acute about March, 1935, and that from this point on the government's re-employment program will be hampered by the lack of materials with which to work, and that the German public will begin to feel actual shortage of a number of articles entering into daily life, such as textiles, metals, fats, lumber, foreign fruits and vegetables, petroleum products, miscellaneous chemicals, etc. The campaign for establishing substitute industries is going on, but these substitutes will most of them be produced at much higher costs than the former imported articles, and the net result must be the freezing of large amounts of capital in enterprises which would be unproductive in normal times and a lowering of the German standard of living.

The coming raw-material shortage, serious as it will be, will be followed by even greater difficulties. The German financial situation is worsening. The banking and credit structure of the country cannot continue to absorb government short-term paper indefinitely. It is now estimated that government employment bills held principally by the banks and to a lesser extent by the Reichsbank amount to about nine billion marks, while the government is ultimately responsible through budget deficits and guaranties for about four billion marks more of additional credits extended, some of them through municipal semi-public institutions, etc. It is confidentially estimated by reliable German economists not in sympathy with the present government that the German financial structure can stand a further increase in government short-term borrowing up to a total of twenty billion marks.

Confiscation of Industrial Capital

An indication of the fact that the government realizes the time limitations on the present policy of re-employment through short-term borrowing lies in the recent announcement regarding the *Pflichtgemeinschaft* or Compulsory Cartel in the lignite industry. This provides for a compulsory contribution from lignite companies of two hundred and fifty million marks for the erection of plants manufacturing synthetic gasoline at an estimated cost of four times the world market price. This illustrates the possibility that the government has in mind a direct confiscation of private capital in order to avoid excessive credit inflation. However, the possibilities in this direction are also limited by the amount of private capital available. The chances are that Germany will move far along the road toward state socialism or state capitalism, whichever we wish to call it, in the next few years.

German Resources Too Small for Population

The essential difficulties in the German situation lie in the physical facts regarding the country. An increasing population of sixty-six million persons accustomed to a relatively high standard of living are now becoming shut off from the outside world. Germany's best assets were her geographical position as a trading and transit nation in the center of Europe, her disciplined and capable workmen and her industrial equipment designed to manufacture foreign raw materials into finished goods for both domestic and export consumption. These assets are largely lost through a policy of trade barriers and political hostility. If the nations of the world are to retire into themselves, adopt a policy of economic nationalism and grudgingly barter their surpluses of certain essential products, Germany is sure to suffer more than most countries. She has only a comparatively poor soil, her mineral resources are scanty with the exception of coal, potash, salt and building stone, her lumber supplies are inadequate and unsatisfactory. She has to offer only the skill of her workmen in manufacturing finished products which are now produced by many other industrial nations and many of which are dispensable, such as toys, glassware, musical instruments, artificial jewelry, etc. Germany's best hope of prosperity lies in a general revival of international trade. If she is to be thrown back on her own resources, her scientists, inventors and industrial organizers must bring into being an entirely new system of synthetic manufactures and must display a skill and ingenuity far beyond anything which the world has known heretofore. In fact, to succeed in this policy, Germany must bring about a whole series of made-to-order miracles and must do it at once. In default of such developments the German standard of living must continue to fall.

Central European War Probable

IV. The eventual end of the National Socialist experiment, whether it comes through a long-delayed internal revolution or whether, as seems much more likely, it comes as the result of a Central European war, will be accompanied by a financial collapse in which liquid capital will be lost and perhaps many existing property rights vanish. As stated above, there are no signs of any successful counter-movement in Germany today, but there are indications that before many years have gone by Europe will again stumble into the expected war, which has already been narrowly avoided several times but which remains just as imminent as before. The pressure of national rivalries and irreconcilable ambitions remains in Central Europe. The various countries are continually shifting and re-shifting their alliances in the attempt to better their relative positions. This results in a relaxation of the tension at one point but a growing tension at another. For example, a year or so ago, the danger point in Europe was generally felt to be the Polish Corridor. Last July, it was undoubtedly in Austria.

There still remain several European countries which are only postponing war until they feel their position is more favorable. No general easing of this tension is possible unless a world-wide economic recovery provides them with a new hope, and relief from their unsatisfactory situation. The chances of escaping a war in Europe rest on the possibility of general business improvement coming from outside, principally from the United States, the British Empire, and, to a lesser extent, from other countries, before some accidental spark is struck which will cause an inflammable situation in Central Europe to catch fire. Meanwhile, Central Europe cannot and will not do its part toward bringing about this improvement in the world situation. All the countries concerned are preparing for a war just as fast as they can. A German businessman reported this week that in answer to a request made to one of the import control offices for a definition of what were considered essential import commodities for which foreign exchange could be allotted, the reply was that only war materials were essential.

American Investments in Germany Bound to Suffer

It is entirely false to believe that war cannot break out in Central Europe because the countries are not financially able to fight each other. A great part of the history of the human race is made up of wars financially impossible to fight. In the next European war, armies may have to live as they have usually lived in the past, off the country. If a Central European war occurs, it looks now as if Germany will be involved and as if existing capital savings will be largely used up in the catastrophe. After reviewing the entire position, it would seem that Americans who continue piling up untransferable mark balances in Germany are going to lose them and that the best German investment for funds which cannot be got out of the country is real property.

25

REGULATIONS OF JULY 29 AND AMERICAN COMPANIES

Berlin, August 9, 1935

As described in our cable No. 3 of July 29, a new regulation became effective on that date, making the importation of foreign goods under the tariff numbers 754-768, 798-800, and 881-925, contingent upon the presentation of a foreign-exchange certificate or an equivalent document. As the Bureau has already been informed, foreign-exchange certificates must be presented to the control offices upon the importation of goods in order to secure payment in foreign exchange then or later. However, a large number of American manufacturers and distributing firms in Germany, who are unable to obtain foreign-exchange certificates for certain necessary imported merchandise, have been willing to bring in such merchandise from their parent companies in the United States at their own risk. Until a few months ago, this procedure went on unchecked. Recently, the control offices have commenced writing letters to American firms who are continuing this practice, advising them that they are subject to punishment under German law if they do not obtain foreign-exchange certificates. Upon receipt of such advice and after consultation with this office, a number of firms adopted the practice of submitting declarations on behalf of the importing firm, stating that payment in foreign exchange would not be claimed. These declarations were considered to be the equivalent of foreign-exchange permits and the goods were legally imported.

Now, however, since July 29, this state of affairs has been changed. Upon inquiry at the customs houses, it appears that customs officials declare that the new regulations are mandatory and give them no discretion, and that they must prove that foreign-exchange permits have been obtained for the goods in question or that barter negotiations have been concluded before allowing imports to come in, provided such fall under the tariff numbers mentioned in the decree. Most of these goods are finished goods of mechanical nature. The tariff numbers under which imports from the United States are listed in the German import statistics for the first six months of 1935 may be consulted, and it will be seen that the items principally affected are automobiles and parts, office equipment and parts, photographic apparatus, agricultural implements, tractors, sewing machines, winding machines, other textile machines, metal working machinery, refrigerators, elevators, leather and shoe making machines, electrical machinery.

Importation of Replacement Parts

There are in Germany a large number of American firms which are manufacturing or distributing products in this category. Most of them have long since ceased importing much in the nature of complete new machines from the United States, but they have endeavored to continue the import of replacement parts to service existing customers. Under the new regulations, they must apparently stop bringing in such parts unless they can arrange a barter deal of some sort, but since these are all highly finished goods, the barter ratio is bound to be set at a very unequal figure, for example, 3 to 1, 4 to 1, 5 to 1, or perhaps even a higher ratio. It is believed that 3 to 1 is about the best that anyone could get. In other words, in order to continue servicing their German customers, these firms must go into the business of exporting German finished goods to a considerably greater extent than the amount of merchandise they are bringing in to Germany. They are practically certain to take a heavy loss in business of this kind.

Loss to German Industry

An examination of this question from a business point of view would indicate that the German economy stands to lose a good deal from these severe new regulations. For example, take the case of the Singer Sewing Machine Company, which has been established here about seventy years and has been manufacturing an immense amount of equipment which is in the hands of German industries, principally the garment trades, the shoe industry, etc. This company manufactures over three thousand separate types of sewing machines, many of them entirely in Germany, but many of them only in other countries. They state that it is an impossibility for them to build and equip plants here to make all the various parts which are needed for industrial sewing machines in Germany, that many of these parts wear out quickly and that within one year, unless they can bring in new parts, their industrial sewing machines here must break down. In other words, the German shoe and garment trades must re-equip with sewing machines of other makes, principally Pfaff and Duerkopp. This will involve immense outlays for new equipment, estimated in the case of one firm (the Salamander Shoe Co.) at eight hundred thousand marks. There are thousands of firms in the same position, though much smaller amounts are usually involved. An American company sells about fifty of their special machines in Germany each year, and two and a quarter million marks' worth of machines are now running in Germany. This company states that there is no other buttonhole machine in the world and that each uniform for the German army, the S.A., the S.S., etc. has had its buttonholes cut on their machines. Nevertheless, last week their shipments of parts were all held up and no way has been found as yet for them to come into the country. In the same way, American automobiles now in the hands of German customers cannot be serviced by the firms that recently sold them. There seems to be little use in making representations to the German government upon this whole matter, as it has been undoubtedly well thought out and is part of a deliberate attempt to drive American companies out of Germany. The authorities are well aware that this represents a considerable damage to a great many German users of American equipment, but on the other hand they see the possibility for large quantities of replacement orders for German equipment and an opportunity for getting rid, once and for all, of American competition inside the country.

One Exception Noted

Since the new regulations have gone into effect, one case has come to the notice of this office where an exception has been made. This was made by the control office for technical products, possibly on the three following grounds. The importing firm obtained a permit to bring through the customs a small quantity of automobile parts on July 31, two days after the regulations went into effect. This was because: (1) the manager of the firm is an old personal friend of Schwarzkopf, the head of the control office; (2) the American firm signed a statement that it would not request payment in foreign exchange in the future, whereas other companies have sometimes only submitted a declaration that they would not request foreign exchange as long as the exchange regulations remain in force; (3) the manager of the company was able to bring to the authorities proof that he personally had been instrumental in obtaining a large quantity of foreign orders for German goods in the past year. It does not seem likely that very many or very important exceptions of this kind will be made or that this one company can continue right along to obtain favors which are denied to their competitors.

Firms Affected

Looked at from a long-distance point of view, it would seem that American firms here, which are prevented from servicing their customers, should probably discontinue their operations and retire from the German market. Any attempt to stay in business on a barter basis would only cost them additional sums of money. Their German competitors are acting as technical advisers for the import control offices and are in a position to administer some more knockout blows in the future in case this one is not sufficient. This office has not yet had time to hear from all the firms affected by the new order, but they will undoubtedly be coming along with the story of their troubles in the next few weeks.

26

EXPROPRIATION OF
JEWISH ENTERPRISES

Berlin, October 23, 1935

EVER SINCE the National Socialist party congress at Nuernberg in September and the proclamation of the anti-Jewish
laws there, a new wave of pessimism and despair has swept
over Jewish businessmen in Germany. The newspapers are
full of advertisements offering Jewish enterprises for sale.
Buyers are few and are able to dictate prices which are only
nominal ones: five or ten per cent of the ordinary value of the
property in question.

In some lines of business, the Jews are definitely forced out
by a certain date. This was the case, for example, on the first of
October for dealers in antiques and art objects, bookstores and
circulating libraries, etc., which fall under the authority of
Dr. Goebbels. In general, however, the Jews are forced out
through general political and economic pressure which is applied extra-legally at this time but which may be given more
definite legal sanction in the specific provisions of the new

anti-Jewish laws which have not yet been made public. It is rumored that a publication of the final text of these laws has been delayed because of differences of opinion between the radical and the moderate members of the party, but that the radicals have in general won their fight to make the new laws severe. It is rumored that the postponed publication may be due to the desire that the United States send representation to the Olympic Games in Berlin next year. While this is under discussion in the United States and not yet definitely decided, the publication of the new anti-Jewish laws may be postponed.

Sometimes Jewish business firms approach American interests as possible buyers for their enterprises and in a few cases American firms have actually become interested. For example, the Adrema Company, owned by Jakob Goldschmidt and his brother Julius, a concern manufacturing addressing machines, has just been bought by the Mercedes Company, which is a local firm owned by an American company. It was also stated yesterday that the N. Israel department store has been negotiating with American interests, and the Grunfeld dry-goods and furnishings store is also looking for an American buyer. Many transactions of sales to German firms are taking place every day. For example, recently it came out that Siemens has taken over the Nora Radio Company. This is a Jewish concern and the name Nora is simply Aron spelled backwards. Siemens has also taken over the Cassirer Electrical Company, manufacturing cables and other equipment, situated in Charlottenburg.

Many of these large Jewish businesses could be taken over for almost nothing. For example, the writer has been approached with the request that he resign from the Department of Commerce service and take over Jewish enterprises in Germany for nothing, with the hope that in years to come he would turn a certain amount of the property back to the original owners who in the meantime would go abroad trusting to the honesty of Americans as their best hope. Several other Americans have been approached in the same way. One such business, which was offered to me for nothing, had a turnover last year of twenty-six million marks. This was a department store concern. It seems unlikely that many Americans, however, will step into such risky enterprises. The chances are that in the course of a few years they would find themselves ousted by the authorities in any case.

Liquidation Possible Only at Heavy Loss

It must be taken into consideration that under present circumstances the moneys which German Jews are allowed to take out of the country are merely a fraction of the actual value which their property represents in Germany. The heavy losses which they incur in this connection result both from the forced conversion of their property into cash in Germany and from the regulations to which exports of these marks are subject.

Jewish *rentiers* are in a comparatively favorable position since in most cases they should be able to turn their holdings of shares and bonds into cash at regular bourse quotations. It should be noted, however, that, as pointed out repeatedly in the German financial press during the last few weeks, these "emigrants' sales" for Jewish accounts were responsible for the drop in security prices since September twenty-second. Owners of real property, industrial concerns and stores are in a still more desperate position. Owing to the mass offering of Jewish enterprises and the lack of buyers who would be able to take over a Jewish firm, prices for such "going concerns" have been extremely depressed. It will be a safe estimate to say that under present market conditions Jewish owners can at best expect to obtain one-quarter to one-third of the real value of their houses, factories and stores.

After having converted their property, whatever it may be, into marks, prospective Jewish emigrants have to pay the capital flight tax (*Kapital-fluchtsteuer*) at the rate of twenty-five per cent of the total. The remaining amount in marks, or seventy-five per cent, constitutes the so-called "*Auswanderer-Sperrmark*," a variety of blocked marks which are today sold at a discount of seventy-three to seventy-five per cent. In other words, the Jewish emigrant with a capital of one hundred thousand marks must first of all pay twenty-five thousand marks in capital flight tax. If he is fortunate enough to find a buyer, he can sell the remaining seventy-five thousand marks at a discount of seventy-five per cent, which would leave about twenty thousand marks at his free disposal, or twenty per cent of the original sum of one hundred thousand marks.

No better commentary on what is going on in the confiscation of business interests could be made than the following translation of an article in the *Voelkischer Beobachter* of today's date (October 23), signed by Nonnenbruch, the economic editor of the business section of the paper:

"Sale of Jewish Business"

"In the process of introducing National Socialism, the Jews step out of business life. The less friction this process brings, the better it is for the National Socialist reconstruction program. The definite effectiveness of National Socialist policy is evidenced by the fact that this withdrawal of Jews from the business world has already occurred to a great extent and that no noticeable disturbances to the economic life of Germany have arisen thereby.

"In the case of small enterprises, such as retail stores, the question of liquidating Jewish interests is comparatively simple. Such German citizens who desire to take over a small Jewish business can approach the *advisory office for retail business sales* which has been set up by the Labor Front. [This office sends out threatening letters to Jewish firms advising them to sell out and stating that they have prospective buyers who are willing to put up sums which turn out to be very small ones indeed. *The writer.*] The *Wirtenschaftspolitischer Dienst* proposes that Jewish sellers in their emigration from Germany should deposit a part of the sales price in Germany, so that out of this sum claims which the purchaser may have against the seller could be satisfied. The possibility that the Jewish seller could take advantage of the German buyer must be completely removed.

"It is naturally impossible that the Jewish seller could take his full pocketbook with him abroad. The lack of foreign exchange forbids that. It is more important for us to make possible the import of raw materials and this lies closer to our hearts than that the Jew is able to take money abroad. Furthermore, the Jews are to a great part, responsible themselves that the easy transfer of their funds into foreign countries has become impossible, since they have carried on the boycott campaign and are actively engaged in increasing the difficulties which are in the way of transferring funds out of Germany. The proceeds of such sales which remain in the country, also remain open to the claims of German purchasers, approved by public bodies.

"In the transfer of ownership of small business properties from Jewish to German hands, the matter then is fairly simple. Retail trade is so well organized that Jewish retail stores do not need to be closed to purchasers in order to secure the transfer of the business. It is difficult in the case of getting rid of Jewish influence in large concerns. Here it is not only the racial but the economic question, for in the first place the possible buyers are the large business enterprises and concerns. These possess the funds for the purchase of large businesses. But is this desirable under National Socialist policy?

"Not at all! In the first place a sale of this kind is handled in this way: The Jewish owner simply transfers a large block of shares. This block of shares then comes into the hands of a German capitalist who desires to control the former Jewish-owned concern.

But blocks of shares are easily transferred. If a factory goes from Jewish into German ownership, then the German ownership shall be permanently secured. But this is not the case when only a block of shares has changed hands. In the second place, it is not good National Socialist policy to increase the power of large business enterprises. We want to see individual businessmen and the greatest possible distribution of business into small hands in which case the single units are made independent or at least remain independent. A Jewish business is a nasty phenomenon, but capitalistic control of factories is another. It would only be half a victory if by the removal of Jewish influence from German business a strengthening of capitalistic influence should take place.

"The purchasing concerns have an interest in the former Jewish factories on account of their own market position. They increase their influence in order to get rid of a competitor. The cost of this must be borne by the workers in the former Jewish-owned plants who will be discharged in part so that the productive capacity of the purchasing company be better utilized. But the German consuming public is not served. Free competition ought not to be weakened in such a case, but should be increased; so that prices can fall.

"So this is the situation. How to operate against it is a question which official economic bodies must solve. Proposals which a newspaper makes are only suggestions as to how the question may be answered.

"The next point is that whoever purchases a former Jewish concern must agree that within a certain period he shall not discharge German workers and employees in the plant which he has purchased. This period of time could be set at two years; because within this period the last unemployed will have disappeared and the right of Germans to work will have become an actual one. In this way, the purchase of Jewish concerns as a method of getting rid of the competition will be prevented.

"A second duty to be laid upon the buyer is that all Jewish employees shall be discharged and their jobs filled by Germans. It is the usual thing today that in plants under Jewish influence many of the important jobs are now held by Jews. If the buyers undertake these responsibilities, then the question of the price at which the former Jewish plants can be taken over is easier to decide. But in such cases it is not only the plant which is purchased, nor with this purchase is it only an advantage in the competitive position which is gained, but the human beings in the plants are taken over and cared for, as well. The purchase is also not a pure capitalistic one and that makes it impossible to look at the purchase price only from a capitalistic viewpoint. [In other words, if all Jews are discharged and all German employees given a guaranty of two years' work, the purchaser should be permitted to take the plant for a song. *The writer.*] The responsibility which the purchaser of the plant acquires toward the employees brings with it the fact that the purchaser shall not use the plant as a mere object of speculation. This means that the block of shares through the acquisition of which he has obtained his influence must be kept in his possession. German economy cannot stand it if large blocks of shares are loosely floating around."

Letter from German Labor Front to Jewish Egg Dealer

The following is a translation, prepared in this office, of a letter recently received by an egg dealer of Jewish extraction from an official of the German Labor Front. It must be remembered that the German Labor Front is a government organization, and the writer of the letter speaks with the authority of the National Socialist party and the German government behind him. The letter is characteristic of the campaign of intimidation, threats and blackmail, with which the German Nazi officials are attempting to drive out of business the remnants of the Jews who are still trying to hold on.

233

"Your letter of the 21st of this month to the chief of the Department of Egg Wholesalers, Eugen Fuerst, has been turned over to me with the request to give my opinion and prepare an answer.

"I wish to state, right now, that it is no part of the duties of the German Labor Front to give advice or guidance to non-Aryans. If, however, I do answer your letter, it is only in the interest of your employees, for I wish to prevent German fellow-countrymen from losing work and bread. For this reason I advise you to attempt to sell your business, i.e., to turn it over into Aryan ownership while this still remains possible; it is well known that with the existing shortage of supplies Aryan firms are given the preference in having their orders filled. In this way, it would also be made possible for your employees to continue receiving wages. Of course, I must reserve the right to withhold my approval of such a sale in order to make absolutely sure that the business actually becomes Aryan. Also, I must reserve my approval regarding the person of the buyer. It will not have escaped your notice that in recent times with the co-operation of the German Labor Front very many non-Aryan plants have been turned over to Aryan control, among them undertakings with a turnover amounting to millions.

"If today, in the entire country, the Aryan import trade and the Aryan wholesale trade refuse to sell to Jews, this is accounted for by various reasons, and there can be no possibility of raising a claim of interference in the business rights of non-Aryans. The unwillingness to deliver goods is based upon the fact that the present foodstuff trade is well aware that for military and political reasons this trade must be in Aryan hands. Furthermore, the supplies of fresh goods are actually very short and one cannot blame the trade if they think first of their Aryan customers. There is no sense in your pointing to the Nuernberg Laws and the regulations which have been published in connection with them. I refer you to the leading article in the *Voelkischer Beobachter* of November 22nd of this year, entitled 'Unwritten Laws.' In recent times it has been repeatedly stated by the Fuehrer and by other persons that the Party rules the State. If a member of the Party enters into business relations with a Jew, he incurs the danger of coming into conflict with the written and unwritten laws of the Party and accordingly of being called upon to assume the responsibility for his acts. Neither the Ministry of Economics, the Agricultural Ministry, the German Labor Front nor any other Government office can compel an Aryan importer or wholesaler today to sell goods to Jewish firms, particularly, in view of the abovementioned facts.

"When you refer to the fact that you were a front fighter, let me remind you in this connection that this was the self-understood duty of every able-bodied man. I have become acquainted with your activities on the front and know that these did not continue for four years, even if you did wear a uniform of a front fighter for four years. Your main service was passed in Belgium behind the lines and in Berlin in the hospital service. You even had the opportunity during the war to look after your business in Berlin.

"Your wish to be allowed henceforth to receive goods cannot be granted on account of the reasons which I have just given. In the last paragraph of your letter you refer to the regulations regarding the citizenship laws of November 14th, 1935, as they affect Jewish officials who were front fighters. This law removes from public employment the last remaining Jewish front fighters, but all of them are to retain their pensions. But you were not an official but are in business for yourself, and revolutions have always had their effects upon certain types of business, and, in this particular case, upon non-Aryan firms in the foodstuff industry.

"I can only advise you to sell your business immediately, as long as it has any value at all; for when you have once lost your customers to those Aryan firms which are able to deliver goods, your business will depreciate or become completely valueless."

"Signed: HOFFHEINZ"

27

HITLER'S DILEMMA

Berlin, October 21, 1937

IN THE AUTUMN OF 1937 German industrial production has reached a new post-war high at fifteen per cent above 1928 figures, while registered unemployed have fallen to 469,000 at the end of September; a new low since the war and which represents only aged, unfit and unemployable persons. From the standpoint of stimulation of industry and solution of the unemployment problem, the National Socialist régime has been more successful than any other government at the present time. How long this success can be maintained partly depends upon how far it was reached on the basis of non-recurring favorable factors and how much of National Socialist practice can be built into a permanent system.

A general statement may be made that National Socialist success in the economic field is a result of exploitation to the full of various situations. Many of these situations are of temporary character. Among such items are the following:

I. *Exploitation of foreign creditors.* In the post-war period large amounts of foreign capital entered Germany in the form

236

of long-term bond issues, industrial participations, stock purchases, and the like. The desire of foreign capitalists to repatriate their funds at any price now enables the German government to profit by the extremely high discounts which it can obtain by selling foreign exchange for marks to foreign creditors. For example, a considerable part of the expenditures under the Four Year Plan has been made possible by the use of such blocked marks, bought at a discount of over eighty per cent. The discount rises to ninety per cent and over in the case of security marks, i.e., marks which arise from the sale of real estate or long-term investments. This robbery of Germany's foreign creditors has been proceeding ever since 1931 and has enabled Germany to acquire title to a large amount of capital which originally entered the country as the property of foreigners. Furthermore, the non-payment of interest on German bonds and the devaluation of the pound and the dollar abroad resulted in large capital gains to Germany.

II. *Exploitation of the Jews.* The seizure of Jewish capital and the driving of Jews out of business and out of the country have resulted in considerable capital gains to the government and to firms and individuals standing close to it. For example, when the Ullstein Publishing Company was forced out of business, the Franz Eher *Verlag*, which is mostly owned by Hitler, took it over at a sum reported to be ten million marks when it was nominally worth one hundred and twenty million marks. The Leiser Shoe Company was forced to turn over majority control of its stock for nothing to a National Socialist firm. These instances could be multiplied indefinitely. Yesterday, for example, an American Jew informed me that he has been squeezed out of his business here and is selling off his remaining funds in Germany (600,000 marks) at less than twenty per cent. His two brothers have already been forced out of the country and have sold off more than a million marks each at approximately the same discount.

III. *Exploitation of German investors.* The issue of government short-term Treasury bills in tremendous amounts for the purpose of financing rearmament, re-employment, and the Four Year Plan, has exploited the German investing and capital-owning class. For example, the mortgage banks, insurance banks and savings banks have been raided and their assets taken over in exchange for short-term paper which is of very doubtful value. Industrial firms supplying goods to the government have been compelled to take their payment in the same short-term paper, only part of which they can discount, and in which form they must retain their profits and surpluses. The German industrial plants aside from those working on war orders have not been able to expend much on replacements or to combat obsolescence since the beginning of the depression which began in Germany ten years ago. For example, in September, 1937, industrial firms not on the preferred list obtained only four per cent of the steel products allotted in the same period last year. It can be assumed that certain amounts were spent in the early part of the depression, namely, in the fall of 1927 and the years 1928 and 1929, but since then practically nothing. In other words, the whole German pre-crisis industrial plant aside from that part working on war orders is running down and its capital value has been partly confiscated by the government.

IV. *Exploitation of natural resources.* Even before the Four Year Plan, government-backed companies were drilling feverishly for all types of minerals and ores found in Germany, stripping the country of its most meager deposits of metals. The new Hermann Goering Iron Works, if they get into full production, can run for only a comparatively few years because the total amount of iron ore in Germany is limited and the construction of the plant will take one-fourth of Germany's steel output for four years, or a whole year's supply. Many of the small mining enterprises, such as nickel, silver, copper, etc., are exhausting such small deposits as have been found in the country. Exploitation of the coal mines is going on at a great rate. Much of Germany's recent industrial expansion has been in brown-coal districts in the middle of the country. The total amount of this type of fuel is only sufficient to run the country for a few years; certainly it will give out during this century. The forests are being cut down twice as fast as they are growing. German farmers are compelled to plant crops to their greatest ability and push overworked soil to the limit. When fertilizer prices were reduced by thirty per cent last spring, it did not mean that farmers could save on their fertilizer bills. They were compelled to spend the same amount of money as before, but to take larger amounts of fertilizer to press more out of the land. In many instances this resulted in souring the land. It may be said that German agriculture has now reached the point where the law of diminishing returns applies.

It is interesting to note that the greater part of German margarine consumption is supplied by whale oil. As is well known, the Arctic whale has been almost destroyed and existing whaling operations are almost entirely in the Antarctic. The Germans are now whaling increasingly and have built new whaling ships; and they, together with the Japanese, are engaging in this new form of fat production in competition with the older Norwegian industry. An attempt by the League of Nations a few years ago to call a halt to the rate at which the Antarctic whale was dying out has failed. It will be only a few years more before this source of supply will be exhausted. There have been many other attempts recently to exploit resources outside the German frontiers, such as sharks and sponges.

Essentially most of these devices of exploitation listed are of a temporary character. Most of them have already passed their peak of productivity. It is obvious that when the German investing class and the foreign bond owners have been completely plundered, there will be nothing more to be gained in this direction. This point lies only a few years ahead.

V. *Exploitation of labor.* But there is another form of exploitation which can continue for an indefinite time, namely, the exploitation of the working class. German wage earners are working on the average of forty-eight hours a week and working with skill and efficiency. Their pay has hardly been raised at all over the extremely low point to which it sank during 1932, while prices of every kind of consumer goods show a slow but constant tendency to rise and are up all the way from twenty-five to fifty per cent above the 1932 level, in spite of official pressure to hold them down. In other words, the working population of Germany is being steadily exploited, for the benefit of the régime, at an increasing rate each year. The only limit to this process is how much the people will stand, and apparently they will stand a good deal. The government is in a position to know how far to go at any time. It can relax the pressure to some extent by slowing down military construction and producing more consumer goods to whatever extent may be found necessary. The German people have completely lost their political rights and it seems unlikely that they can, by their own efforts, escape from the trap into which they have fallen.

Temporary Remedies for Permanent Problems

Strangely enough, the government itself has fallen into a trap as a result of promising more at the beginning than anyone could possibly perform. Hitler got his power originally as a sort of miracle man. He promised to solve the unemployment problem and he did so, but he solved a permanent problem by the use of only temporary remedies. With the exhaustion of Germany's capital resources and raw materials, and with the excuse of rearmament less effective, the task of keeping the unemployed at work becomes more difficult every year. In other words, Hitler has raised Lazarus from the dead but he now has to keep him alive without having much to feed him.

Drive for Colonies

Hitler also assumed power under the force of the belief that he was going to reverse the decision of the war and give Germany back her former place in the world. This is somewhat vague. Sometimes it appears to refer to the position which Germany had under Bismarck, but more often to the Hohenstaufen Empire of the Middle Ages. At any rate the ideal of Pan Germany or Greater Germany has been set before the minds of the public; and this particularly includes colonies. In the last few weeks the German newspapers have been engaged in a storm of protest, complaints and wails regarding the loss of Germany's colonies and the necessity for their return. The Four Year Plan has been almost forgotten in this propaganda drive to which Hitler has personally lent his support and for which he has definitely risked his own personal prestige and that of the National Socialist government. Every day that this continues commits the government more firmly to obtaining a success in this field or suffering a humiliating setback. Unfortunately for the Nazis, the same irresponsible hesitation and inertia abroad which ordinarily prevent resistance to German demands, now offer the severest obstacles to Hitler's success in his colonial campaign. For one thing, there is no concrete opponent whom Hitler blames and nobody on whom to land blows. Hitler is shadow-boxing on the colonial question now and is just wearing himself out without getting any tangible results.

Partial Solutions No Real Help

To sum up the present position of the German government, it is forced to assume responsibility for continued successes in the field of foreign politics and continuance of full employment and industrial production inside the country, while at the same time its own economic policy is destroying the invested capital of the upper and middle classes, a situation which is abhorrent to Hitler and his friends and particularly to the army. This situation cannot be cured by small remedies. For example, the conclusion of a trade agreement with the United States would give Germany a little relief in getting raw materials, but would only slightly slow down the rising cost of living and the progressive lowering of the standard of living. A devaluation of the mark would have practically no effect on the whole situation. Its only relief would be to reduce the levy on business firms for the maintenance of the export subsidy, but this would be balanced by the fact of rising domestic prices of imported goods with new threats to the cost of living.

Colonies No Great Economic Advantage

The reacquisition of pre-war German colonies, at least those which would seem most likely to be given back, namely, Togo and Cameroon, possibly Southwest Africa, would be an immense psychological and emotional lift to the government and the German people. It would provide them with something to talk about, brag about, and keep busy about for quite a while, but its effect on the supply of raw materials and the standard of living would be negligible. The kinds of material Germany needs cannot be secured in quantities from any of her former colonies—not petroleum, metals, textile materials, lard, grain.

The acquisition of such colonies would immediately call for large capital expenditures in the form of shipping, railways, road construction, buildings, agricultural and mining machinery, and many other things. How Germany, which at present can hardly get on with the Four Year Plan for lack of steel to build the new factories, could develop colonies at any speed, seems a problem. The acquisition of colonies would also call for increased naval expenditure to defend them. Hitler's whole contention is for equality of rights for Germany. He would certainly want to make his colonies militarily impregnable through fortifications, naval bases, colonial armies, increased battleships, submarines as well as planes, or else come into complete dependence upon British good will for the retention of his colonial assets. This raises the question whether it would not be good politics for the British to urge certain colonies of low value upon Hitler in order to keep him in a dependent position—and whether Hitler would dare accept colonies on such a basis. At any rate, it seems clear that the German people are going to be disappointed in their present hopes of an improved material position through colonies.

Germans Accept the Inevitability of War

Hitler then has risen to his position of vast power on the basis of the implied promise that he will continue to achieve the impossible both in domestic economics and foreign expansion. Is this situation going to drive him into war? Certainly at the end of 1937 the older generation of Germans do not desire war any more than they have done in previous times. Nor does it seem likely that responsible officers of the army wish for any general European war. However, the irresponsible youth of the country, with its career to make, is talking and thinking about war continually. The public has heard so much about it that practically everyone has come to accept the inevitability of war. The country as a whole has not grown fonder of war, but it is becoming by insensible degrees more resigned to the idea that war must come. It is upon this basis that the boys of today are planning their own lives. They are not studying hard in school or looking forward to a career in business, but are principally thinking about army promotion as a career. The German public does not consciously feel that they are quite sincere. They are very vague about who will actually start the war. However, across the frontiers there is no vagueness at all. Every other nation in Central Europe is convinced that war is coming and that Germany will start it, and they are all bending their whole energy to protect themselves in such an emergency.

Germany Unprepared for a New World War

There is no doubt whatever of the immense potential strength of Germany in any war, or of the effectiveness of such troops as she has already been able to train and the supplies and equipment she has already accumulated. Germany is, of course, better able to win a short war than she ever was, because her motorized striking columns could be more overwhelmingly superior at the outset than were her troops in 1914. It is difficult, however, to see how Germany could stand a prolonged general European war in view of her lack of foodstuffs and critical industrial raw materials. Dr. Schacht's weekly, the *Volkswirt*, ran a series of articles this summer in which it was pointed out that a major power would need about twelve million tons of petroleum per year to conduct a first-class modern war and that only the United States and Russia, and possibly the British Empire, are in a position to obtain supplies of this magnitude, whereas the German consumption of petroleum, now about five million tons a year, is more than fifty per cent based on foreign imports. These conclusions lead one to believe that Germany does not desire a major European war or even a war with Soviet Russia, with all the risks of long lines of communication, heavy consumption of materials and drain of manpower.

It seems much more likely that Hitler hopes to obtain some colonies by a combined process of bluff and bargain, and some continental addition to Germany through short military action similar to the Italian success in Abyssinia. It is for this purpose that he is maintaining a common aggressive front with Italy and Japan. In fact, the success of the Italians in Abyssinia, the drive of the Japanese into China proper, and the campaign of Franco in Spain are all based, in the last analysis, on the existence of a rearmed Germany. Otherwise none of these projects could have been successfully accomplished and would not even have been undertaken.

Japan and Italy Acting Too Quickly for Germany

Hitler is in the position of being potentially the strongest of all the aggressive states, but not the nimblest. While he frowns and menaces, his fellow gangsters are taking advantage of the moment and filling their pockets. It seems possible that, if this goes on a year or two longer, Hitler will be confronted by a very unpleasant dilemma, namely, that in the case of both Italy and Japan, either success or failure will make them less valuable partners for any common campaign to give Hitler his share. For if the Japanese and Italians succeed in winning new territory and prestige they will need Hitler less, will want peace and relaxation of tension in order to develop and organize what they have won. If, on the other hand, they lose or at least fail to win, they will become so deeply involved and weak that they will be of little use to Germany when her hour has struck. In other words, the timing has been bad for Hitler.

Some Action Indicated—But What?

This would seem to indicate that he should act before very many years go by. And yet the grain harvest of 1937 was disappointingly small, not only in Germany but in other Eastern European countries through which he might like to march. The German reserves are not yet adequately constituted. Hitler needs several more years to wait for a favorable grain harvest, train a few more classes of reserves, swell his officer corps to the necessary proportions and perfect his mechanical equipment, synthetic production of petroleum, synthetic rubber, production of steel from low-grade iron ores, and synthetic textiles. Certainly nothing has been left undone that could have been done to prepare the way for an immense German military effort. If nothing comes of it, the result will be an anticlimax and a disappointment for millions of young and ardent spirits. Germany will have to readjust herself to make the best of what remains from the lost opportunities for peace, but with her capital largely frozen in military preparations. It is not human nature for a country to come so close to a great effort and then fail to undertake it.

End

BIBLIOGRAPHY ON "RACIAL SCIENCE"

AUTHOR	TITLE
Prof. Dr. A. Basler	*Einfuehrung in die Rassen-und Gesellschafts-Physiologie*
Paul Brohmer	*Biologieunterricht und voelkische Staat*
Ludwig Ferd. Clauss	*Rasse und Seele*
R. Walther Darré	*Das Bauerntum als Lebensquell der nordischen Rasse*
Egon Freiher von Eickstedt	*Rassenkunde und Rassengeschichte der Menschheit*
Friedrich Wilhelm Prinz zur Lippe	*Vom Rassenstil zur Staatsgestalt*
Dieter Gerhart	*Kurzer Abriss der Rassenkunde*
M. R. Gerstenhauer	*Rassenlehre und Rassenpflege*
R. Goldschmidt	*Die Lehre von der Vererbung*
Dr. Hans F. R. Guenther	*Adel und Rasse*
Dr. Hans F. R. Guenther	*Der Nordische Gedanke*
Dr. Hans F. R. Guenther	*Rasse und Stil*
Dr. Hans F. R. Guenther	*Rassengeschichte des hellenischen und des roemischen Volkes*
Dr. Hans F. R. Guenther	*Rassenkunde des deutschen Volkes*
Dr. Hans F. R. Guenther	*Rassenkunde des juedischen Volkes*
Dr. Joh. Hartmann	*Rassenpflege*
Otto Kleinschmidt	*Rasse und Art*

E. Meyer—W. Dittrich	*Erb- und Rassenkunde*
Alfred Rosenberg	*Der Mythos des 20. Jahrhunderts*
Dr. Bruno K. Schultz, Zentralinstitut fuer Erziehung und Unterricht	*Erbkunde, Rassenkunde, und Rassenpflege* *Erblehre—Erbpflege*
Paul Schultze—Naumburg	*Kunst und Rasse*
Prof. Dr. H. W. Siemens	*Vererbungslehre*
Martin Staemmler	*Rassenpflege im voelkischen Staat*
Otto Steche	*Gesundes Volk, Gesunde Rasse*
Erich Voegelein	*Die Rassenidee in der Geistesgeschichte*